The Sc Governors' Handbook & Training Guide

Second Edition

Tyrrell Burgess & Anne Sofer

Kogan Page

First edition 1978 entitled *The School Governors' & Managers' Handbook & Training Guide*
Second edition 1986
Both published by Kogan Page Ltd,
120 Pentonville Road, London N1 9JN

British Library Cataloguing in Publication Data

Burgess, Tyrrell
    The school governors' handbook & training
    guide. — 2nd ed.
    1. School management and organization — England
    I. Title   II. Sofer, Anne
    379.1'531'0942   LB2901

    ISBN 1-85091-117-7

Printed and bound in Great Britain by
Billing and Sons Limited, Worcester

The School
Governors'
Handbook
& Training Guide

Contents

Part 1: Governors' Handbook

Part 2: Governors' Training Guide

Preface

This book is intended first as a handbook of information and suggestions for governors of schools in England and Wales, and second as a guide for the training of governors. The handbook should be of use to all practising governors and others who want to know how the education system works: it is also an essential element in the training scheme we outline in the guide. The training scheme itself should be useful to any instructor or teacher in college, school or institute who wants to mount such a course or any group of governors who want to help themselves. This second edition has been revised to take account of changes since the book was first published in 1978.

None of it could have been written without the help of the members of the committee of the National Association of Governors and Managers who helped us to devise and run the course and advised us on the content of the handbook. In particular we should mention Winifred Tumim who helped us with the section on special schools, and Stanley Bunnell and Tony Travers who constructed and piloted the secondary school mock agendas. To all these people we are immensely grateful, as we are to the organisers and participants of the courses for governors we ran in many parts of the country during the period we were writing this handbook; those at the University of Loughborough Summer School and the ILEA's City Literary Institute were particularly helpful.

We should also like to acknowledge with thanks the permission of the Inner London Education Authority to quote a section of the Auld Report, and use their plans for a nursery class; and finally the permission of the Controller of Her Majesty's Stationery Office for permission to reprint the extracts on pages 93 to 106 and the table on page 88.

Part 1:
Governors' Handbook

Chapter 1

Introduction

Governors are an important part of the education system. They should represent different elements in the immediate community, and act together as a link with the community and a support to the school. They are also the local body to whom the head and staff are accountable for the 'conduct and curriculum' of the school, and are required to participate in many important decisions in the school's life.

The following pages are a guide to the various duties and responsibilities of governors and how to fulfil them. Governors can only carry out their formal duties *corporately* – ie they can only take decisions and initiate action through resolutions passed at a properly constituted meeting, or through their chairman acting under delegated power. The early part of this guide therefore concentrates on the business of the meeting, so that you will know how to use these occasions usefully. However, the wisdom and effectiveness of your corporate actions will depend very much on the strength of the relationship that individual governors have built up with their schools and the understanding they have developed of their needs and problems. The latter part of this handbook therefore broadens out into advice on visiting the school and developing this relationship.

In recent years there has been a growing interest in the functions of governors and the way in which they are appointed. The National Association of Governors and Managers, which directly inspired this handbook and training course, was established in 1970 to press for reforms and to improve the effectiveness of governing bodies. Many local education authorities began to change the composition of governing bodies by making provision for the appointment of parents and teachers. In 1977 the report of an official committee of enquiry (the Taylor Report) recommended governing bodies representing equally the local authority, parents, teachers and the local community. The Education Act, 1980, was the Government's response to these recommendations. Since then there have been proposals for increasing parental participation.

It is important that governors are aware of the issues that have been debated, so we have thought it right to retain in the book a summary of the Taylor proposals (with the NAGM response) and add a summary of the latest Government proposals. It is also significant that the changes which are being made and proposed are not so much a radical departure from previous arrangements as a revitalising and strengthening of them. The 'spirit of Taylor' can be achieved within existing arrangements, and throughout this book we have tried to show how governors can act effectively, whatever their particular circumstances.

Chapter 2

How Did You Get There?

The first formal notification that you have become a governor will probably be a letter from the Director of Education (or Chief Education Officer as he is sometimes called) of your local education authority, or from the clerk to the governing body. Before 1980 people appointed to secondary schools were called governors, and those appointed to primary schools were called managers. There was no difference between their functions and both are now called governors. You may still come across the term 'manager' in books or documents written before 1980, and we have not changed such historical documents where they are quoted in this book.

You may very well know some time before you receive this letter that your name has been put forward. If you have been elected to be the representative of the parents or teachers, then it will only be a formality to have your nomination ratified by the Education Committee. Nevertheless, even formalities take time, and as a result you may miss a meeting. If you know you are to be a governor and have not received formal notification after a week or two, or if you know there is a meeting coming up (the head of the school can tell you this) phone the education office, ask for the section dealing with governors and find out what has happened to your nomination.

If your name has been put forward through some other body – a local political party or community group – it may be that this is only a first stage nomination and that someone higher in the organisation, or at education committee level, is selecting from among several nominations. In this case, if you hear nothing for some weeks, contact the body which originally put your name forward and find out what has happened.

When you get your letter of appointment, you will probably also be told the date of the next meeting. You may not have to wait until that meeting before visiting the school. Most governing bodies adopt the practice of allowing their members to arrange visits individually with the head; but you should make sure (by asking the head) that this is acceptable before making an appointment. Your 'right' to visit the school depends on the corporate decision of the governing body, who may have instituted formal arrangements for doing so: if this is the case you will have to fit in with these arrangements until you can persuade the governing body to change them. Suggestions about how to visit a school and what to look for are in Chapter 15 on Visiting the School.

Many people wonder how others get to be governors. Many governors themselves are vague about the process, and even those who know about their own appointment may look round at their fellow governors wondering about the process which brought them there.

Perhaps it is comforting to know that your position as a governor is firmly rooted in the law. Section 17 of the Education Act, 1944, says that for every county school there shall be an 'instrument' providing for the constitution of the body of governors of the school, and this instrument is made by order of the local authority. (In the case of voluntary schools the instrument is made by order of the Secretary of State.) So the first thing to do is to look at your school's instrument of government. You should have been sent one of these on your appointment as govenor and if you have not, write to the Director of Education to get one.

You will see from the instrument that the governing body has to consist of a stated number of people. These may be appointed in different ways:

1. Some will be appointed directly by the local authority: they may be councillors.
2. Some will be parents, appointed by the authority after an election among all the parents of children in the school.
3. Some will be teachers appointed by the authority after an election among all the teachers at the school, (or members of the non-teaching staff similarly elected by their fellows).
4. Some may be pupils appointed by the authority, perhaps after an election among the pupils at the school.
5. Some may be co-opted by the other governors.

The balance among these five groups is laid down in the Education Act, 1980. There must, for example, be at least two parent governors and one teacher governor if the school has fewer than 300 pupils and at least two teacher governors if it is larger. There are some authorities which have more parents and teachers than are specified in the Act, and a few authorities have pupil governors. In a rather larger number of schools pupils are invited to attend the governing body as observers.

The position of the head teacher may differ from one school to another. Under the 1980 Act he can elect to be a governor *ex officio,* but he can also decide not to be. Some heads feel more comfortable if they are regarded by other governors as the 'chief executive' of the school, rather than as a fellow governor.

It is usually clear how the parent, teacher and pupil governors come to be appointed: they are elected. The election of parent governors may be done at a parents' meeting, or there may be an elaborate ballot through the 'pupil post'. The election of teacher governors is usually quite straightforward.

The way the local authority itself appoints governors is less obvious. Usually, the political parties represented on the authority agree to divide the places among themselves in proportion to their strengths in the authority. Thus the majority party will have a majority of the places appointed in this way on each governing body. Nominations come through the local party organisations. The surest way on to a board of governors if you are not a teacher or parent at a particular school, is to be active in one of the political parties or have friends who are. Many local authorities would claim that the appointments made in this way need not be of politically committed people, and indeed some have made conscious efforts to go outside narrow party nominations. But in most, the situation is as described here.

There is a complication in primary schools, in that where there is a 'minor authority' (like a district in a county) that authority may appoint at least one governor.

In a voluntary aided or special agreement school the foundation governors outnumber the other members of the governing body by two if there are 18 or fewer governors, and by three if there are more. At least one of the foundation governors must be a parent. In a voluntary controlled school at least one-fifth of the governors are foundation governors.

The co-opted governors are often local worthies (the vicar, perhaps) but where political control is thought to be important they may be simply members of the majority party chosen by that party's majority on the governing body.

The rest of the instrument provides for detail like the financial interest of governors, the filling of vacancies, the election of chairmen and the conduct of meetings.

There is one person who will appear at governors' meetings and who may not be mentioned in the instrument of government, and that is the clerk. Usually, the clerk is an official representing the Director of Education. In some cases he will merely take notes and forward resolutions to the appropriate offices. In others he will act more positively as a spokesman for the education authority, explaining policy and procedure. The clerk can be an extremely important influence on the proceedings – for good or ill. Sometimes he can be very effective at preventing discussion of awkward issues and frustrating action. On the other hand, a helpful clerk can be invaluable in suggesting possible courses of action and pursuing the governors' complaints and resolutions with energy. It is well worth making a friend of the clerk and encouraging him to take an interest in the school, seeing that he is invited to functions and so on as a matter of course.

In some authorities, and in voluntary schools, the clerk is not an official of the education department but is appointed by the governors, either a volunteer from among their own number (sometimes called a correspondent) or some other person, often the school secretary. The advantage of governors appointing their own clerk is that they feel assured of his support and independence from the bureaucracy. The disadvantage is that such a person will probably be less knowledgeable about local authority business and may not know how to forward the governing body's requests and proposals. If your clerk is appointed by yourselves, it is worth checking that he has clear lines of communication to a helpful official of your local education authority.

Before you go to your first meeting you should certainly read the instrument of government carefully, together with any explanatory leaflet you have been sent. If anything is not clear ask the chairman or the clerk.

Your first meeting may be a little bewildering, and you may not know exactly who is who. This will depend on what sort of arrangements for welcoming new members are made by the body you have joined. If you feel they are inadequate you might suggest at some point, for the benefit of future new members, that an opportunity be made for the governors to meet informally, either before or after the meeting, so as to get to know each other. Some governing bodies make a practice of doing this either at every meeting, or once a year, sometimes inviting the staff to join them as well.

Chapter 3

What Are You For?

Once you have discovered who you and your fellow governors are, and how you came to get there, the next thing is to decide what you are there for. Again, your functions are rooted in the law. Under Section 17 of the Education Act, 1944 (as amended by the Education Act, 1980), every county school must be conducted in accordance with articles of government. These articles are made by the local education authority, but the articles for secondary schools have to be approved by the Secretary of State. The articles of a voluntary primary school are made by the local education authority but those of a voluntary secondary school are made by the Secretary of State.

Section 17 says that the articles of government 'shall in particular determine the functions to be exercised in relation to the school by the local education authority, the body of governors and the head teacher respectively'. In short, it is the articles of government which tell you what your responsibilities as a governor are. These may vary from one authority to another but they are likely to include some responsibility for finance, school premises, the appointment and dismissal of teaching and non-teaching staff, the organisation and curriculum of the school and the suspension of pupils. Each of these points is dealt with in later chapters.

For the present it is enough to say that a newly appointed governor should study very seriously the articles and any explanatory notes the authority sends with them, so as to be sure of his precise responsibilities. As we shall see later, even the most vague or limiting articles can be used for the benefit of the school if governors are prepared to think about them and use them.

It may be worth adding that the functions of governors are of different kinds. One of these functions is that of decision. In effect governors decide when they are appointing staff or are considering the suspension of a pupil. Both these actions may require the confirmation of the authority, but initially the governors decide. A second function is that of recommending that the local authority should do something. This function covers the governors' role in approving estimates and in keeping an eye on the state of the building. Here the governors do not have power directly to decide what is done: what they have is the power to recommend and to urge their recommendation. A third function is that of overseeing what goes on in the school. The governors' responsibility for conduct and curriculum comes under this heading. In carrying out this function the governors are the body to whom the head and staff are accountable for the conduct of the school and all that goes on in it. The head is responsible for the management and organisation of the school, and of course the staff carry professional responsibility for the education of pupils; so it is

15

for the governors to represent the public interest by receiving reports, by asking questions and making comments and suggestions. The fourth function is that of representing the school in the surrounding community, helping to give the school a sense of separate identity and purpose and standing up for it if it is in trouble.

These functions are interrelated. For example, it would be hard for governors to make intelligent appointments (which is something they have to decide) if they had been excluded from their responsibilities for the conduct and curriculum of the school. But it is worth being sure what kind of function is involved when you are discussing a particular issue at a governors' meeting. It will help you to realise quite quickly what powers and duties you in fact have and what you can reasonably expect to achieve.

Do not forget that your own place and function are part of the wider spread of responsibilities. You are appointed by and are responsible to the local education authority. This is the council of the metropolitan district, non-metropolitan county, outer London borough or the Inner London Education Authority. Each of these, by law, has to have an Education Committee – so you might hear it referred to as 'the LEA', 'the authority', 'the council', 'the committee' or even 'Croydon' or whatever the authority is. The council is, of course, the members, the councillors, elected by all of us. The permanent officials are the Director of Education and his staff, and you may hear them referred to as 'the director', 'the CEO' (chief education officer), 'the office' or County (or City) Hall.

The authority has different responsibilities from your own. For example, it must provide schools and see that these buildings are up to standard; it must make your instrument and articles of government (if yours is a county school); it must assess which children need special educational treatment; it must see that parents carry out *their* duty to see that their children are educated; and it must adequately provide further education and appoint a chief education officer. In addition it *may* do a number of other things, such as establishing and maintaining new schools, controlling the appointment of teachers and secular instruction, causing its schools to be inspected, assisting research and buying land by compulsory purchase.

A local authority cannot do anything unless it has the specific power or duty to do it – and very few of them try. If you do not like what they are doing you will normally have to rely on persuasion and pressure.

The responsibilites of the Secretary of State for Education and Science are different again. The Secretary of State (now sometimes called the Education Secretary) is a member of the Government and is responsible to Parliament for the education of the people and the development of the education service. To help him or her there is a department of the Civil Service, the Department of Education and Science, known as the 'Department', 'the DES', or 'Elizabeth House' (the head office in London). Broadly the Secretary of State regulates: ie sets the context in which local authorities provide, either by laying down standards (as for school premises) or by announcing policies and, as a last resort, legislating for them (as with ending the 11 plus examination).

More recently the Secretary of State has taken a growing number of initiatives which affect the work of authorities and schools. Currently the largest of these is the 'Technical and Vocational Education Initiative', which is funded through the Manpower Services Commision. There is also central funding, known as 'Education Support Grants', for educational priorities listed by the Secretary of State for Education every year. In 1985–86 one of these priorities is courses for governors.

Local education authorities have to put in a bid for specific schemes under both these arrangements. Obviously not all bids are successful. Some authorities so dislike this new and more centralised method of funding that they refuse to bid. Governors will have their own views on this; but they should feel free to ask the local authority what Government funds are available and what its policy is in relation to them. If they feel there is some source of money which the local authority is not tapping, they are entitled to argue their point.

On some occasions decisions of the Secretary of State may directly affect your school, for example on school closure or on new building, but normally they will influence the school indirectly. This does not mean that you do not have access to the Secretary of State. Anyone can write to the Secretary of State, and you can specifically complain, under Section 68 of the Education Act, 1944, that your local authority is acting unreasonably – and anyone can complain about you as governors under the same Section and on the same grounds.

Chapter 4

The Agenda

Before you come to your first governors' meeting, you will almost certainly have been sent some papers. These will include the minutes (or record) of the previous meeting, and an agenda. This is to tell you what is going to be discussed. (An example is on page 124.)

The agenda is a list of items, and may have attached to it a number of papers with further explanation about individual topics. The word agenda means literally 'what is to be done', and the thing to remember, as you consider each item, is, what are we going to do about this? There are several kinds of things that can be done. On some items the governors may decide something. On others they may simply hear a report and comment. Sometimes they will want to exercise a pressure, on the authority or in some other direction. So the first thing to get clear is the kind of action which is appropriate.

The second thing to realise is the way in which things are done in committees. If there is a general discussion which ends without a decision being taken, nothing will happen, however good the discussion or however much the committee is agreed. The only way to make something happen is to pass a resolution. The governors may resolve that the headmaster should seek the views of the staff about the school meals provided and report back at the next meeting. A resolution may be generally agreed or it may be a matter of controversy. If there is disagreement, the chairman will put it to a vote and it may be carried or lost by a simple majority. So as each item is being discussed ask yourself what you want to happen as a result of the discussion and make sure that a resolution is framed accordingly.

It is also important to decide what kind of resolution is required. Many boards of governors, like committees in general, pass resolutions that are simply expressions of opinion. The governors deplore or regret or congratulate. There are some occasions (as with congratulations) where this is all that is necessary but it is important to remember that expressions of opinion carry no consequences. A board of governors is part of a bureaucracy, and in a bureaucracy if you want something done you have to give somebody the job of doing it. So if it is action you require your resolution would ask the local authority, or the clerk, or the head to do something. Unless you specify what you want done and specify who should do it, you can be sure that nothing will happen.

Let us now turn to the agenda. With a new committee the first item will be the election of a chairman. In those authorities which control the political composition of governing bodies, you will probably find that all this is fixed beforehand. (In a few authorities the chairman is even formally appointed beforehand.) Somebody will smoothly move Mr So-and-so, who will be elected without a vote in conditions which look like apathy. In fact this is the opposition members accepting the inevitable with as good a grace as they can muster. Where the balance of the parties is very narrow, it may be that the opposition will take advantage of absence on the other side to nominate one of their own people and get him elected. This always causes bitterness. With the appointment of parents and teachers to governing bodies, there may be a loosening of political control. In these circumstances any govenor can think of the person who might best be chairman. If you wish to propose someone, you must make certain beforehand that he is ready to stand. If you do not do this, your nominee may back out with embarrassment all round.

New governors often feel left out of their first chairmanship election, but there is no very obvious remedy for this. You can try ringing up your fellow governors and sounding opinions, or you may feel bold enough to suggest to the outgoing chairman that an informal get-together before the first meeting might be helpful so you could get to know each other. It is probably only realistic, however, to accept that it will be difficult for you to achieve much before your first meeting. In most authorities there is a re-election of the chairman and vice-chairman annually. A note on the duties of a chairman appears at the end of this chapter.

After each reconstitution of the governing body – ie every four years in most cases – there will, in those authorities where this is the practice, be an item on the agenda to consider the co-option of additional governors. In some cases the majority political party may come along with prepared nominations which their numerical strength will enable them to vote in, but this is not by any means always the case, and it is well worth while giving a little thought to this matter before the meeting, and having ready some nominations of people whom you feel would be useful additions – people within the community of importance to the life of the school whose voice might not otherwise be heard on the governing body: local employers or trade unionists, or members of ethnic minority groups, for example.

Another early agenda item is the minutes – the record of the previous meeting. These are kept by the clerk and should be circulated beforehand. The purpose of the minutes is to ensure that the governors and the authority know about, and can check back on, what the governors have decided to do. It is therefore very important to see that the minutes are right. If you think that any minute misrepresents what was said or done, you should say so. If most of the governors agree with you, the minutes will be changed. Minutes can be presented in a number of different ways. In some places they are a record of decisions only. In others they record what was said as well as what was decided. The former practice is preferable, because unless literally everything is written down, there is bound to be some element of selection and people are bound to be misrepresented. There is a useful compromise in which minutes consisting wholly of decisions may record one member's specific objection to some proposal if he requests it.

After settling that the minutes are right, the next job is to check that what was decided at the last meeting has actually been done. The agenda heading here is 'Matters Arising from the Minutes'. If the last governors' meeting called for a report, then the report should be available and should appear later on the agenda. If the clerk was asked to provide some information he should provide it. If the matter arising is substantial, it will appear as a separate item on the agenda. If not it can be dealt with on the minutes themselves.

There may also be in some authorities an item called 'Delegation of Functions'. This is the occasion when the governing body as a whole is asked to decide which of its number can carry out some of its functions without referring back. It is important to be quite clear who is authorised to do what. Do not let this item be hurried through as a formality; make sure everybody understands what it means.

Another recurring item at the beginning of the agenda will be an account of the action taken by the chairman, for which he will seek the governors' approval. This is dealt with in the note at the end of this chapter.

After the item on chairman's action the agenda will contain specific reports and other items which are dealt with separately in this book. There will, however, be a number of routine items at the end of the agenda which should also be mentioned here. One of these is the date and time of the next meeting. This seemingly innocuous item can have important consequences. For example, some governors are in the habit of meeting at times which make it difficult for working people to attend. Normally, the clerk will try to find a similar time and place next term to those of the meeting you are currently attending. You may not be able to manage that particular day – and of course it is hard to please everyone – but if you find the time proposed is generally difficult, do not be afraid to raise it. Governors do change their habits, and there is no reason why they should not be asked to discuss the convenience of their meeting times.

In this context it is worth knowing that Section 59 of the Employment Protection Act, 1975, entitles an employee who is a governor of a maintained school or college to 'reasonable' (but unpaid) time off, to attend to the duties this entails. If the employer refuses to grant it, the employee can complain to an industrial tribunal. This Section came into force in April 1977, and the interpretation of 'reasonable' has not yet been tested, but we would judge that it should certainly include termly and emergency meetings of governing bodies, and probably a regular visit as well. More guidance about this is contained in the Department of Employment's leaflet No 12 in the Employment Act series called *Time off for Public Duties,* which is available free from any of the Department's jobcentres.

In many agendas there is now an item on confidentiality. Here the governors will be asked to decide which if any of their discussions should be regarded as confidential. This item assumes extra importance when there are parent or teacher governors, because these governors will want to know how far they can report back to the people who elected them. Practice differs from one place to another, but probably a good rule is that the governors should make as little confidential as possible. The less confidentiality there is, the more likely it is that confidential items will remain so. A normal practice is to keep confidential anything that directly affects individuals – like the suspension of pupils. There is no reason, however, for keeping confidential the posts and salaries of teachers. These are public matters, and there can be nothing confidential about them (although details of what happens during interviews and the subsequent discussion *should* be kept confidential).

Finally, there is 'Any Other Business'. In some authorities this is quite specifically called 'Urgent Business', and this underlines the purpose of the item. You should not try to bring up under Any Other Business anything that occurs to you. The reason is that the agenda exists so that everyone who has a right to attend the meeting knows what is coming up and can prepare if necessary in advance. It would be very unfair to those who are absent if any item of importance arose of which they did not have prior notice. If something of this kind is raised, a good chairman will ask that it go on the agenda at the next meeting. It is preferable, if you have something to raise, that you should raise it on an earlier item on the agenda – say the head's report. After a little practice, you will find that there is almost nothing that cannot be raised as a relevant point on an agenda item.

If you feel that what you have to raise demands a full discussion on its own, then ask the chairman in advance to put it on the agenda for the next meeting. If for some reason the chairman will not put it on the agenda, see if the head will propose to him that it be discussed. (The chairman may be more willing to listen to the head than to a fellow lay governor.) If you get no response here either, and you still feel it is important, you can propose formally at any appropriate moment during the meeting that the subject be discussed, either at that meeting or at a future meeting. Make sure you have a seconder in advance, if you can. If the matter is disputed the chairman can put to the vote whether it be discussed or not. The chairman or clerk may try to argue that the matter is not within your competence as a governing body. Check with your articles beforehand that you will be able to justify raising it under a specific clause, and have the document with you. If you are sure of your ground but are ruled out of order, you can write to the Chairman of the Education Committee of your local authority for guidance.

This is the correct formal way of proceeding. However, although it is important to know these steps, you may decide that a confrontation of this sort is better avoided and that your purpose will be better served by proceeding with more diplomacy and attempting to bring up the subject which worries you under another guise, and under another heading. If it is genuinely important it will not go away because the chairman decides on one occasion to avoid it, and a campaign of polite persistence may win through in time.

Once there has been a vote on any issue, that is binding on you. You have no decision-taking, policy-making functions as an individual governor (unless under 'delegated powers') and cannot act independently or as an unauthorised group of governors. However, one initiative you may be able to take is to call a meeting of the governing body. You will have to check with your own instrument on this point; many instruments allow a meeting to be called by any two governors. Normally, of course, you would ask the chairman to call a meeting if there was some special reason, but the power to do so yourself with only one ally is useful to know about.

So much for the agenda. New governors may find it rather formal and bewildering. Perhaps the best remedy for this is to take advantage of your ignorance. Do not be afraid of asking simple questions. You will find that there are many other governors who also want to hear the answer, but who thought that the question was too simple. You may even find that it is the simple question that reveals the most inadequate answer. When you gain confidence, you may wish to probe more deeply, but even here an assumption of ignorance can be a help. Heads, clerks and chairman may take offence at the aggressive enquiry, and may be disarmed by a very similar question couched in terms of a simple request for information. The important thing is to find out, not just to irritate.

Try not to forget, either, what your purpose in finding out is. There is no point in pressing hard for information if neither you nor your fellow governors are going to do anything with it. It is your duty to know what is going on in the school, but that does not mean you have to ask lots of disconnected questions about everything under the sun. It is a good idea to concentrate your efforts. Indeed, it is probably a good idea to decide before the meeting just which of the items you yourself are going to pursue. You will almost certainly be better at dealing with these if you are not at the same time trying to do everything.

In all this, try to see that you are properly serviced. If the head is going to make a report to the governors, particularly if it is full of facts and figures, you can reasonably insist that he puts the important detail in writing and circulates it beforehand. Few people can react intelligently when faced with a quarter of an hour's recital of attendance percentages. The head should be asked tactfully to do the governors the courtesy of preparing a proper written statement for them in advance. Similarly, the clerk should be asked to produce all the relevant papers in good time for those items on the agenda which require it. In the last resort, you ought to refuse to discuss an item if you have a feeling that you have not had a chance to get a proper grip on it.

The Chairman

The chairmanship of the governing body is a genuinely important post. The most visible part of his job lies in chairing the meetings and, probably, chairing speech day if there is one. The chairman can make an enormous difference to the effectiveness of a governing body, to the speed with which it conducts its business, to the pleasantness of the meetings and to the consequences of the discussion. In some ways he can determine whether the governing body is a help or a hindrance.

The clue to effective chairmanship lies in sticking to the agenda and making sure that the governors are actually discussing something and know what this is. On any important item, the governors, like any other committee, may want to talk round the subject in a general way for a little while. If this goes on too long, however, the governors lose track of what they are doing and the discussion becomes unproductive. The chairman's job is to remember that the governors ought to be discussing what is to be *done* and that they do this by passing a resolution. What he should try to do therefore is to get someone to propose a resolution to form the basis for the discussion. This will concentrate the governors' minds and lead to some action.

Of course, it helps if the chairman is well versed in the general rules for the conduct of business, like how to deal with amendments, and so on, but if the chairman is clear about what he is doing he will be able to manage the meeting whether or not he knows precisely about the rules of order.

Equally important are the things the chairman does which are not so visible. Because the governors meet infrequently the chairman acts for them between meetings, not only in being available to the head for advice, but in pressing the authority on many of the other things the governors would take up if they were sitting constantly. In many authorities he effectively makes staff appointments, or sits on the authority's committee which appoints the head-master. So when you elect a chairman you are electing not only the person who runs the meetings but also the person who acts for you between meetings.

An account of the action taken by the chairman will be on the agenda at every meeting, and the chairman will seek the governors' approval for what he has done. Normally there will be little that is controversial here: the chairman will be acting within well defined limits of local regulation and convention. Nor does any chairman act better for constant sniping at governors' meetings. But you should take the item seriously, and not just act as a rubber stamp. You can ask any questions that occur to you and you can very often provoke an important general discussion (say about methods of appointment) on this item. It may be that you have a chairman who has got above himself, and has taken a lot of decisions that were not particularly urgent and which raised general questions: these you may feel he should have left for the governors to decide. If you have such a chairman you and your fellow governors may have to spend some time making clear that you think he is going too far.

It is also possible to have a chairman who, on the contrary, does too little. If this is the case he will need tactful urging both at the meetings and in between them to act more vigorously. If you feel he should be pursuing a particular line of action, for instance in making personal representations to the Chairman of the Education Committee to ask for some long-deferred improvement in the school, make this suggestion at the meeting and try to ensure it is agreed and minuted. Then you can ask about it at the next meeting under Matters Arising.

Chapter 5

The Head's Report

The head's report to the governors should be the real matter of the meeting; it is the formal occasion at which the head gives an account of his stewardship and the governors fulfil their duty of overseeing the conduct and curriculum of the school. However, actual experience does not always match this theoretical picture. It is a not uncommon complaint that the head's report, often occurring at the end of the agenda, can be both delivered and listened to somewhat perfunctorily, and appears to be no more than a catalogue of visitors and visits, and successes in the swimming gala and daffodil-growing competition.

If you feel that this is happening at your school, there are several things you can do. You can ask the clerk if the head's report could come at the beginning of the agenda, and this should cause no problem. You can also ask for it to be typed and circulated before the meeting, so that you will have a chance to study it.

A number of heads, however, do take the report seriously. It is pre-circulated and it contains such items as figures of attendance, details of examination results, figures of reading attainment, disciplinary problems and new curricular developments. It is the governors' duty to discuss and question all these items. On figures of attendance and examination results, for instance, you can ask for a comparison between this school and the local average. It is possible these figures may not be available, and if they are not you can press the authority for them. Some authorities, sometimes under pressure from the teachers' organisations, are unwilling to make this sort of information generally available, on the gounds that comparison between schools' performance unrelated to other factors such as socio-economic background of the intake is meaningless and misleading. You must make up your own mind on this point, and perhaps suggest ways in which more meaningful information *could* be compiled.

What should be suitable for comparison are figures for past years, and these may in fact tell you more: any improvement or deterioration should be noted. You can also ask for a breakdown of the figures you are given. Which year group's attendance record is best and worst? Which departments have most exam entries and most exam successes? This may uncover policy decisions, or even discrepancies in policy-making, that it is the right of the governors to know. Some subject departments, for instance, may believe in entering the whole ability range for examinations, others may enter only the most able. There may very well be a justification for this, and the governors can perform a useful function in giving the head and his staff an opportunity for explaining why things are organised in this way. On the other hand it may be an anomaly which has never been thought out, and in this case the governors may be useful in provoking the realisation that this is the case.

If you are on a governing body where some of these topics are never mentioned in the head's report, you can ask that they should be. If you are not sure how your request will be received, it may be wiser to approach the head privately about it, suggesting that the matter would be of interest to the governors. If the request is refused, it is open to you to ask for the subject to be put on the agenda: this request should be put to the chairman and the clerk. Obviously, it is up to individual governors how (and whether) they attempt to get change on these issues, and Chapter 16 on Public and Private Pressures suggests some of the possible approaches.

However, even if you cannot achieve the changes you think would be beneficial in the way in which the head reports to the governors, it is still possible to make the most of even the most seemingly trivial head's report. Almost any event in the school's life raises wider issues than are immediately apparent and can be the occasion for questions that confront these issues. If, for instance, the head reports that Miss X has been on a course on the teaching of reading, a governor can inoffensively take this up and ask about the quality of the course and of the authority's in-service courses generally. Are there enough? Are they useful? Do the school's teachers feel well-equipped to teach reading? Do we have enough suitable books? Good contact with the local library? General questions of this sort about provision may lead naturally to the more delicate ones about performance: how well are our children reading? How does the school go about assessing how well they read? On the other hand the manager who is pursuing this subject may choose *not* to take the questioning this far, but may just express general interest and ask for a further discussion at another meeting.

This suggestion – of a particular curricular area being discussed at each governors' meeting – will probably not offend the head or teachers, particularly if expressed by the governors as a desire to be informed, and may go some way towards meeting some governors' frustrations about the lack of serious discussion of educational matters.

Similarly, reports on school visits and competitions can be followed up by questions which relate to the philosophy of the school generally. Which children are chosen to do what is often a good indication of the priorities of the head teacher (or whoever else in the school makes decisions). Therefore the questions, 'How many children were involved?' and 'How were they chosen?' are crucial.

The last paragraphs may suggest that we regard the head's report as an opportunity for intensive cross-examination. Although alert questioning *is* part of the governors' duty, it is not by any means the only reaction called for from them at this part of the agenda. They should also be ready to give thanks and congratulations, support or advice. It is very important that governors should congratulate the head, or ask him to pass on to a member of staff their congratulations, for any significant achievement, whether it is an academic triumph or success in helping a disturbed child. Similarly, if the governors are invited to look at the work of a group of pupils (for instance an account of a school journey) it is important to do it seriously, and again, to use this opportunity to discuss the educational objects of the particular exercise.

Part of the head's report may deal with difficulties he is facing of communication with other agencies – with the Education Office, the Architects' Department, the School Meals Service, the Educational Welfare Service, the evening institute that shares the same building, and so on. It may be that he feels that a governors' resolution about something will get him results, or it may be that in a more general way he wants a concerned audience before which to express a grievance. It is the governors' duty in this case to try and get to the bottom of the problem of where the communication has broken down (it may in fact be within the school) – and suggest how it could be put right. Sometimes the chairman may take the initiative in suggesting a meeting at the school with the other party (architect or social worker or principal of the evening institute) in order to straighten out the situation. On other issues it is sometimes useful to set up a small sub-committee or a working party. Such a group can work more quickly than the whole board of governors and this practice also has the advantage that it is a good way of involving new and enthusiastic governors in a specific task.

We have given examples of the sort of educational and administrative issues that are likely to come either under the head's report or as separate items on the agenda. These are dealt with in subsequent chapters.

Chapter 6

Accommodation

Problems connected with the actual buildings of the school may sometimes appear to dominate governors' meetings. A good chairman should be able to prevent the discussion from getting bogged down in a lengthy discussion of nagging detail, but his whole area is very important: the damage that can be done to the quality of life in a school by a poor standard of maintenance and by delay and difficulty in getting urgently needed improvements is great, and governors have a direct duty to do something about it.

There are three categories of building works that take place in a school: maintenance, minor works and major works. The maintenance of the building and of its heating and lighting are part of the running costs of the authority and it has a duty to keep these to a proper standard. Minor works are projects costing under £120,000 and can be anything from the simple installation of a sink in a classroom to the building of a small separate block. Major works are projects costing over £120,000. The authority annually submits a list of its major projects to the Secretary of State for Education and Science, with an estimate of the total amount of money it thinks will be necessary. The Secretary of State then informs the local authority what it is *allowed* to spend (which may very well be lower than its 'bid'). It will probably recommend that within this figure the 'minor works' element should not amount to more than a certain percentage. To get a building project approved by the education committee for submission to the Secretary of State is therefore by no means a guarantee that it will actually be programmed. The Secretary of State can also sometimes announce special building programmes for specific purposes (for instance secondary re-organisation).

Maintenance

The governors' duty with regard to maintenance is spelled out in most articles of government: 'The governors shall from time to time inspect, and keep the local education authority informed as to, the condition and state of repair of the school premises.' This of course does not mean that you do not expect the local authority to inspect regularly; and you would also expect the head and the caretaker (sometimes called the 'schoolkeeper') to keep their eyes open, notify any defect promptly to the proper authority and pursue the notification with reminders until the job is done. The governors' job is to ensure that this process works smoothly, and to use pressure when it does not.

If you find there is great delay and inefficiency in getting repairs done in your school, you should start by finding out what the system of notification is – who gets in touch with whom, and how? The caretaker is the crucial figure here and it is important for governors to get to know him and involve him in their discussions. In a few authorities he may sit on the governing body, either in his own right or as a representative of the non-teaching staff; in others he may be invited to the relevant part of the meeting. In any case in your visits to the school you can ask to meet the caretaker, and make it clear that you recognise his importance in keeping the school functioning smoothly.

It is possible that the fault in notifying repairs lies within the school. Do all the teachers know what they are supposed to do about things that are not working properly? Are the lines of communication and division of responsibilities between head and caretaker clear? Is the caretaker persistent enough in badgering whatever department it is to get an urgent job done quickly? It is not necessary of course to cross-examine all concerned to find out this information. Often simply asking to have the system explained will highlight where it is breaking down.

More often the breakdown in communication lies outside the school – in one office or other of the authority or with a contractor. If you suspect it is in the office, you should ask the clerk to explain to you the system of maintenance and repairs, which department is responsible, and how you, the governors, can get in touch with them. You can ask for a site meeting which one or more governors would attend with the officer – probably in the Architects' Department – who should be overseeing the work.

Sometimes the fault lies not so much with any department but with the whole system. There may be a policy to let some items of maintenance mount up and be done when the school is due to be decorated, for instance, or there may not be a sufficiently close check on the list of approved contractors. In cases like this the governors should press the authority to adopt a better system.

Some articles of government give governors 'power to carry out urgent repairs up to such an amount as may be approved by the Local Education Authority'. If you are given such powers, find out the mechanics of how to use them. Sometimes they are so complex as to discourage schools from taking this sort of initiative, and if this is the case you can ask for the system to be explained clearly. You can also press for the amount of be raised: it was probably fixed at a time when building work cost half what it does now.

In recent years, some local education authorities have cut back heavily on maintenance, rewiring and redecoration budgets, which has caused a serious deterioration in the conditions of school premises. If you feel this is the case in your authority, ask for the budget figures for the last few years and check whether they have in fact kept pace with inflation. You can also ask whether the painting and rewiring cycle has been lengthened. Every year, Her Majesty's Inspectors issue a report on the effect of government expenditure policies on educational provision. This is available from HMSO. It does not reveal particulars about any named authorities, but it will be useful background reading for any probing questions you decide to ask.

Minor Works

Minor works money will be used either for additions to the school or for internal modifications. More and more as old buildings are being turned to new uses, adaptations are needed. If the head and staff of your school are anxious to convert part of it so as to make it serve the children's education better, it is worth asking them to prepare a paper for the governors' perusal, and then for forwarding to the authority, which sets out clearly the educational needs and advantages of the proposed solution. Governors who have a particular interest or expertise in the use of buildings could offer to come in and discuss the matter with the head and whatever teachers are involved: although the professionals will know less about buildings or have less of an 'eye' for the possiblities than some members of the governing body. If it is an ambitious or complicated scheme the authority's architect should be asked to advise.

Governors are often told by the head teacher and staff that there is a desperate need for more accommodation in the school. When they visit they may be aware of crowded classrooms and the inconvenience of multiple use of halls and dining areas. Before demanding extra accommodation, however, it is worth doing some homework and having a well documented case. The local authority is not going to be impressed with the need for an additional classroom for instance if the class size in your school is considerably smaller than the average for the area generally.

There are several facts it is worth finding out if you want to make out a case for extra accommodation. First are the numbers on the roll and the rate at which the roll is changing. If the roll is growing simply because the school is becoming more popular and recruiting from a wider area, then the authority's only action may be to do something about the school's admissions policy (see Chapter 13 on Admissions), but if you can establish that the growth has come from within the school's normal catchment area, this will carry weight. The authority will probably have had some sort of projection from the Planning and Housing Departments of the council on which it is basing its provision. You, as governors, should ask to see this projection and assure yourselves that it does in fact give a complete picuture of developments in the area.

Another piece of research well worth undertaking is an investigation of how adequately your school matches up to the Education (School Premises) Regulations 1981.[1] These regulations are made by the Secretary of State and specify, for instance, the minimum size of classrooms and school sites, and the minimum number of lavatories etc appropriate for each category of school. It is the duty of the local authority to see that their schools conform to these regulations, although there are circumstances in which the Secretary of State can give directions that substandard premises shall be 'deemed to conform', where it would be impracticable or unreasonable (that means usually, too expensive) to require conformity.

If, therefore, you find, on checking your school against the Education (School Premises) Regulations that it has a grossly inadequate site, and a shortage of certain specific accommodation required, this does not necessarily mean that the local authority is breaking the law. You should ask, however, when the Secretary of State's direction (that the substandard premises were to be 'deemed to conform') was made, and how long it is anticipated that it should remain in force. It is possible that this may shame the authority into doing

---

[1] Extracts from the Education (School Premises) Regulations 1981 are quoted on page 93. The whole document can be found in *The Law of Education* by Liell and Saunders, (Butterworths) available in public libraries.

something sooner rather than later to improve its school premises, or may strengthen its hand in persuading the Secretary of State to allow it to spend more money on building and improvements.

Often governors' requests for more accommodation are met with the answer, 'Your case is a good one, but there is no money.' It is true that spending on building is controlled by the Secretary of State so that even an authority that wants to make improvements may be thwarted. However, it is always worth pursuing your claim, and trying to get it a place on the authority's programme, however pessimistic the authority is about the chances of its being reached in the near future. When the government does decide to release money for public building work, it often does so suddenly and wants the money spent quickly. Therefore any scheme which is prepared and ready to go out to tender is likely to get done. The governors have an interest in seeing that their scheme reaches this stage.

Agitation for more or improved accommodation may sound like a lot of work for governors. It *is* one of the cases where it is worth setting up a working party to find out the facts and document the case quickly. It is also one of the cases where the skills of members of the governing body can be made use of if, for instance, you have any surveyors, architects or builders who have the expertise to suggest to the authority how the necessary improvements might best be made. However, it should not be assumed that a lot of time and expert advice must necessarily go into the job of putting a case to the authority. The authority, after all, has its own professional advisers, and it is up to the governors to make proper use of them; for instance, to ask the authority's statisticians to produce their evidence of population trends, and the authority's architects to inform the governors how far the school falls short of the DES standards.

Major Works

Some schools, of course, do in fact get completely rebuilt. This may not necessarily happen as a result of pressure from the governors; it may be as a result of policy to replace certain sorts of building. If you are told that your school is going to be rebuilt, do not assume that you cannot look a gift horse in the mouth. It is important to make sure that everyone connected with the school is asked to consider what sort of new building is needed if at all. Some primary schools have found out rather too late that the old 'three-decker' Victorian building was more spacious and, if imaginatively remodelled, more flexible, than the new open-plan construction built cheeseparingly to the early 1970s cost limits. Even though the cost limits (by which the DES controlled the amount that could be spent, per child, on new school buildings) have been abandoned, economic stringency is likely to be such that space standards and extra amenities will be cut to the bone, and it would be as well for governors to enquire closely into what the new building will provide before they accept the offer too joyfully.

However, once it is decided that the school is to get a new building or if you have succeeded in getting a substantial extension, it is important for the governors to make sure that parents, teachers and other users of the buildings are consulted before the architects' brief is prepared. Too often the governors are simply presented with the plans for approval, and it is very difficult for a lay body at this stage to judge how far the plans – which usually need a fair degree of technical ability to decipher – represent a building which will be appropriate. The proper stage for governors to be involved is in making sure that the teachers, parents and community in general are taken seriously as 'clients' before the building is designed.

If, once the building is designed and the plans presented (and you do manage to interpret them) you feel that the scheme is a bad one, you should not be inhibited from expressing your misgivings because you feel it has gone too far to be changed. The authority will probably try to tell you that if the scheme has to be redrawn it will mean that it will 'lose its place on the programme'. However, if there are widespread and serious criticisms it is probably worth risking this delay. If you show determination, the authority will almost certainly find the time.

Other Uses of Buildings

One more duty of the governors should be mentioned under accomodation – the use of the school premises out of school hours. Often the articles give governors some control over this although usually the proviso that it is 'subject to the direction of the local authority' effectively curtails it. This whole area tends to be fraught with controversy and tension. There is sometimes appalling under-use of school premises, and governors may feel that as representatives of the community they should press the claim of particular goups that badly need accommodation. On the other hand, some school buildings' capacity is stretched to its limit, and an authority's apparently laudable policy of making its premises available to all comers may lead to severe strain on the schoolkeeping staff, both in cleaning the building/and in making it secure. If you, as a governor, feel you want to effect some change as regards out of hours use, whether it is to increase or to limit it, there are two things you should do: first you should have a clear picture of what the timetable of usage is, and how it compares with other schools; and second you should try and ensure that the several users have some opportunity of knowing each other and discussing their joint problems. Too often joint users only know each other through complaints on the telephone or in writing. Your authority may be thinking of introducing a scheme whereby all users are represented on the same governing body – or on each other's governing body. This is one way in which communication can be improved. You could also take the initiative in proposing a joint meeting, preferably informal to begin with, if no other machinery for contact exists.

Chapter 7

Finance

The three main components of an education authority's spending are: employees' salaries, debt charges on building loans, and running expenses. The only part of all this that appears in the form of estimates before the governors is, in most authorities, that part of the running expenses that is concerned with furniture, books, equipment and expendable material. This is usually covered by what is called the capitation allowance, ie an allowance of so much per head (per pupil), and this is discussed in more detail below.

The Total Estimates

In some areas the governors do get to see the total estimates for the school, which have usually been prepared by the authority's officers. The preparation is based on formulae already approved in most cases by a sub-committee of the Education Committee. For the authority the individual estimates for a school come at the *end* of the estimating process. For the school, they mark the beginning of planning for next year.

There are a number of things that governors can do with the estimates. They can challenge individual items and maybe get some immediate small concession or alteration. More important, governors can see for themselves where the bulk of the money goes and can guard the public's interest in seeing that value is gained for it. They can see the consequences for an individual school of the prior decisions of committees and, if necessary, they can work to change the decision on the basis of experience. An alert governing body can be a great help to a school in this way by making the authority face the consequences of its actions and improve upon them. Maybe a formula should be altered, or differently applied. Only experience can help to decide.

Local Authority Budgets, and How Governors Can Influence Them

Even though actual figures may not be presented to governors as estimates, the governors are concerned with and can influence spending. They can do this largely by well-informed pressure. Specific recommendations on teaching establishments and accommodation are contained in the chapters dealing with these topics; to apply pressure in these and other areas it is worth knowing a little about how the education service is financed.

Local authority services (including education) are paid for out of a combination of the rates and a grant which the central government makes to all local authorities, called the rate support grant. (There is also some income from fees, loans etc.) About half of the money spent by local authorities in the country as a whole in fact comes from the central government. The way this is distributed to individual local authorities depends upon a complicated formula which includes a subsidy to domestic ratepayers (you and me), an attempt to increase the resources of poor authorities, and some calculation of the authority's 'spending needs': the two latter comprising the 'Block Grant'. The Government now also uses this Block Grant to discourage authorities from spending above a centrally set assessment of spending need (the 'Grant Related Expenditure Assessment' – GREA) by tapering off grant as spending exceeds the GREA. This system is amended and recast almost annually. What is more, the Government has taken further powers to limit the rates of some or all authorities – commonly known as 'rate capping'. These new measures mean that although a local authority may claim to be constrained by the Government, which may indeed be true, it still does not mean that the authority has no discretion on spending within an overall total.

The local authority associations negotiate with the central government over the distribution of the rate support grant, and individual local authorities decide on the amount they have to raise from the rates when they know what the rate support grant is going to be in general and will mean for them in particular, usually in December or January.

The framing of the local authority's budget for a particular financial year (beginning in April) takes virtually the whole of the preceding year. In the early summer the 'spending' departments of the authority, like education, will be working out how much money they need (a) to maintain the service at its present level; (b) to accommodate the consequences of developments already in hand (like staffing for a building which will be completed during the year); and (c) for new developments on which the Education Committee has decided or may decide. If a development requires money it cannot start unless it is allowed for in the estimates. The 'spending departments' will also be aware of the possibilities of cuts in expenditure arising from Goverment pressure through the Rate Support Grant or from the policies of the council itself.

During the autumn the education department is faced by the finance department with the amount of money that is likely to be available, given the outcome of the rate support grant negotiations and the readiness of the council to raise the rates. There is an inevitable period of trimming and pruning the estimates. Early in the new year, the estimates are finalised and the level of rates is decided. Even then the estimates are vulnerable to uncertainty about the amount of grant to be paid out.

The lesson for governors is that if they wish something to be done for the school that involves money, they must be sure to get it into the estimates at the appropriate time. This means that if something is to appear in the year beginning next April, the governors will have to have made their point probably by the summer and certainly by the autumn of the current year.

It is also important for governors to inform themselves about any special funds the authority has. It may be that your school could claim for a needed improvement under one of these. Some authorities are informative about their special funds, others fairly secretive. If you can get no useful information from the officers, ask your councillor to find out, if necessary by a question in the time allowed for this at council meetings. In recent years these special funds have become more significant as a hedge against the uncertainties of Rate Support Grant.

Your articles may appear to give you more power in financial matters (for instance the power to inititate the estimates for the school year) than appears to be used in practice. Wise local authorities, however, do not ignore the general influence of governors and the pressures they can bring to bear, in framing their budgets. We know of one local council which decided to make a fairly severe cut in its education budget; the Education Committee (perhaps not as committed to this policy as its parent body) circulated all its governing bodies with a document analysing what this would mean in each individual school, and inviting them to choose between various options. The resulting outcry from governors (who were also in most cases ratepayers) succeeded in reversing the policy.

Capitation

The financial item that is most likely to appear before the governors is a proposal for the spending of the capitation allowance. The estimate usually appears before the governors broken down under such headings as: apparatus, consumable materials, library books, other books, prizes and major equipment. By the time the governors see the figures it is sometimes difficult to do anything but rubber-stamp them. However, there are some useful points to be made.

The governors should certainly feel free to ask for items, particularly 'major equipment', to be broken down and particularised. The head teacher should then be prepared to justify his decisions.

The head teacher, or the governors, may or may not be allowed freedom within a total capitation budget. The capacity to switch resources from one 'head' of expenditure to another or within an amount under a single 'head' is called the power of 'virement'. If the head teacher or governors do not have this power, it is worth pressing the local education authority for it.

If the head has discretion to distribute the capitation allowance, it would be right for the governors to take an interest in how – by what processes of consultation within the school – decisions are reached on the allocation of resources. It is possible for considerable tension to develop in a school if, for instance, a head decides to spend quite a large proportion of the school's capitation on an item of equipment for one department without due consultation with the others. If such a dispute comes into the open at a governors' meeting it is possible that more consultation will take place next time.

The governors can scrutinise the balance of spending between the various heads and compare it with previous years. In a period of cutback in public spending, or when the price of paper, printing etc is rising faster than that of general items, it need not be seen as cheeseparing or niggling for governors to look carefully into wastage, and also possibly into alternative (or supplementary) cheap sources of supply.

In all this it is important to remember that the capitation allowance is certainly part of the head's responsibility for the 'management' of the school (see the articles of government). He presents them to the governors as a courtesy. The governors' duty is to look at the implications of what he is doing for 'conduct and curriculum'. How is the distribution done? What are the educational consequences?

What governors need not do is concern themselves with the auditing of the accounts. This is done at the education office. (Those that take their responsibilities particularly seriously can check that this is so.) In any case, usually the money never passes through the school; the school simply has the right to indent for the agreed items of expenditure.

Voluntary Funds

However, this does not apply to what is often called the 'school fund', ie the unofficial fund made up of voluntary contributions, proceeds of jumble sales etc. This fund is usually under the control of the head, though the authority may provide for an audit. Some authorities insist that the governors of each school see and approve this account, but in the majority the school fund is regarded as no concern of the governors. One line of action, therefore, for governors who want to assume more responsiblity for the school's finances, is to urge the authority to make the overseeing of the school fund the responsibility of the governors of the school.

What is essential is that the governors should be aware of any proposals for spending the school fund which may make later demands on the capitation allowances. It may not be right to look a gift horse in the mouth, but there are no rules against wondering how much it will cost to feed.

New Developments

In recent years a few authorities have sought to give more reality to the governors' financial responsiblities and to enhance the managerial responsibilities of heads. The most fundamental change proposed is by Cambridgeshire County Council. As this book was being revised Cambridgeshire was deciding the generalisation to all secondary schools of a pilot scheme of local financial management. Under the scheme the county council would distribute a lump sum annually to each secondary school on the basis of a formula related to the numbers and ages of pupils in the school. The school would then prepare its budget which it would notify to the council and would be required to manage its affairs in accordance with its budget. There would be full virement between heads of expenditure and both over- and underspendings would be carried forward to the following year. The county council would provide heads with a monthly computer printout of their income and expenditure under the detailed budget heads.

The pilot scheme has shown that heads welcome the additional responsibility. Of course, the changes that can be made from year to year are normally marginal, because the bulk of expenditure is already committed, but these marginal changes, consistently applied, can quickly assume considerable significance for the running of the school. Day-to-day management becomes simpler, more rational and less subject to delay.

A significant aspect of the pilot scheme has been the involvement of governors. From the beginning the Review and Evaluation Group for the scheme has comprised the heads and chairmen of governors of the participating schools. Within the schools the scheme has been managed by finance committees of governors and staff.

Schools and authorities wishing to explore the possibility of devolving financial responsiblity in this way should certainly study the Cambridgeshire scheme. (See *Financial self-management in schools: the Cambridgeshire scheme* by Tyrrell Burgess, Working Papers on Institutions No 53, October 1983, North East London Polytechnic.)

Chapter 8

Appointments

One of the most important jobs that governors do is to make appointments of staff. How many governors are involved in each part of the process varies widely from authority to authority. There will certainly be something in your articles on this subject, perhaps giving you general responsibilities, perhaps outlining the process in some detail. If you feel that the process as laid down is unsatisfactory, then you must put pressure on the local authority to change it, either through a resolution of your governing body, or through any other group to which you belong. In the case of primary (county and voluntary) and special schools, the articles can be changed by a resolution of the local authority; in county secondary schools any change the local authority wants to make has to be approved by the Secretary of State. Voluntary secondary schools' articles can only be changed by the Secretary of State.

You may find that the articles give you certain duties in respect of appointments which are in effect delegated, either to the head or the chairman or a small sub-committee. A decision to do it in this way must have been taken by the governing body at some stage, and can be changed by a vote to do so. If you feel the arrangements need reviewing, canvass opinion among your fellow governors informally, and then propose to the chairman that the governing body has a discussion of the matter.

There are usually three stages in the appointment of a teacher. First, an advertisement is placed either in the local authority bulletin, or in the national educational press. Framing this advertisement may be a simple matter, but for some jobs, particularly at a higher level, the governors may feel they want a hand in it: the tone, style and qualities stressed in the advertisement could attract or deter the sort of candidate they feel the school needs. If an important job is coming up, you can ask who is drafting the advertisement and when it is appearing. The governors can then resolve, if they so choose, to recommend to the authority that certain points be emphasised. (This does not mean that the authority will necessarily carry out this advice or that the governors have power to compel them to do so: that depends on their articles.)

The second stage in the appointment is the shortlisting of applicants. This can be the most important stage, and one in which most governors are in practice not usually involved. If you have a general discussion of appointment procedures on your governing body, do not forget to discuss this step as well. Again, if it is an important job, in particular a headship, it is essential to have a full discussion of what the school needs by the entire governing body, so that those governors who are delegated to attend the shortlisting (if there are any) can bear the views of the entire governing body in mind.

The third stage is the interviewing of shortlisted applicants. This may seem a frightening prospect to new governors. Unfortunately, few governors have the experience or knowledge of interviewing techniques to match their undoubted desire to do the job well.

There are, of course, well established interviewing techniques which have been developed in industry and elsewhere. Many governors would be embarrassed and awkward in following these techniques to the letter, but their basic principles are essential to all good interviewing. The key to the process is that all concerned should know what they are doing. In an interview you need to know, first, what is the nature of the job to be done; second, what is required to do it well; and third, which of the candidates best displays these qualities.

The interviewing panel should not begin to see the candidates until it has made up its mind on these three questions. To be courteous, the candidates should be called at some stated time after the time at which the governors meet, so that the governors have plenty of time for a preliminary discussion.

In discussing the job to be done, you will look at the advertisement that was placed for it and any material on the job that was sent to the candidates. You can ask the head and any inspector present to enlarge on these responsibilities and to tell you about any informal activities which are not mentioned in the formal terms of reference. You and your colleagues should then try to agree on what determines whether such a job is being well done.

You can then move on to discuss what such a job would require in terms of qualifications, experience and personal characteristics. Agree, if possible on those qualities that would rule someone out as well as those that would suggest his appointment.

You are now ready to decide how to judge whether or not each of the candidates before you possesses the qualifications, experience and characteristics required. Much of this, like qualifications and experience, can come from the application forms. But further information about experience and almost all information about personal characteristics will come from your questions at the interview.

When the interviewing panel has reached agreement, but before the candidates come in, each interviewer should have in front of him a list of things that he needs to know about the candidate but cannot get out of the application form, report, references and so on, to use as a checklist as the candidate replies in the interview.

When the candidate comes in, try to make the atmosphere as relaxed and pleasant as possible. This is mainly the job of the chairman, but all governors can contribute – if only by smiling as the candidate sits down. Remember you are trying to judge how well the candidate would do a job, not how well he performs at this interview, which is an artificial situation he is unlikely to need to face very often in the job itself.

Be economical in the use of interview time. The information that needs gathering is that which will be relevant to your final decision. Before putting any question to a candidate ask yourself, 'What information do I hope to get out of the answer to this question?' and 'What conclusions shall I be able to draw from the various possible replies?' One useful way of find out about candidates is to ask them questions about how they approach particular relevant problems in their present job. Most people say that they can make better comparisons if they ask all the candidates the same question: they then have some base from which to judge the replies. But remember that an identical question can affect different candidates differently; for some it may be easy, for others awkward, so you should try to detect this and allow for it.

Do not forget that the object is to make an appointment, not to draw up an order of merit. If there are six candidates, the decision that matters is who comes top and gets the job and who comes next. The order of the remaining candidates is irrelevant.

Do not forget too that even the most considered questions may still fail to give some candidates an opportunity of displaying their strengths. The chairman should certainly encourage every candidate to add his own statement at the end of the governors' questions, or to make any point that he feels has been insufficiently brought out. There should also be time for the candidate to ask questions of the governing body.

Remember that the information you get at an interview is never all that there is to know about a candidate. You have to judge from what you see about a whole lot of things which you do not see. In particular, social poise and articulateness are impressive at an interview but may be less important for doing the job well than other qualities such as sympathy and understanding, which are not so obvious in an interview. In the interview you are seeing the candidate relating to people who are formally his superiors; do not forget that for teachers a more important quality is the ability to get on with colleagues and pupils.

If you have prepared well for the interviews in your initial discussions, the final decision should be relatively easy. Do not forget that one option open to you is *not* to appoint. The job can be readvertised. This can cause delay, but may be worth it. If you do decide to appoint, the successful candidate should be asked to return and offered the job. Usually the governors will require an immediate decision on acceptance; indeed the candidate's presence at interview must be held to imply a willingness to take the job if offered. It is a useful practice for the chairman to ask, at the conclusion of each interview: 'Are you a serious applicant for this post? Would you take it if it were offered?'. Then at least you know if any of the applicants' acceptance is in doubt.

It is very important that unsuccessful candidates should be treated courteously. The chairman of governors should be asked to see these candidates, to thank them for coming for an interview and to wish them well.

Of course, the interview is only part of the process of appointment. Arrangements should certainly have been made to enable any candidates from outside the existing staff to see the school in operation and to discuss it and the job with the head and other staff. You are not appointing a new member of staff in isolation. You need to know how any candidate will fit in with the existing staff, and you need to know, for example, how far a decision not to appoint an internal candidate will affect the morale of the school. You may decide to appoint from outside regardless, and in many instances it may be right that you should, but you ought to do so aware of the consequences.

You will usually find that there is a specialist or general inspector or adviser sitting in on the appointment to help you. He or the clerk may read out confidential reports or, in some authorities, open reports on the candidates. Confidential reports are usually read after the candidates have been seen, and this can be unfair in that the candidate does not know about and does not have the chance to answer an unfavourable report. Open reports, on the other hand, may very often be simply bland and may in the event be supplemented verbally by the inspector with what is in effect a confidential report. The way to cope with this is in the initial discussion, where you have decided what it is you are looking for. You can then take from either confidential or open reports the information you require, and are less likely to be swayed by irrelevancies.

It will also be the task of the inspector or adviser to sum up for the governors the strengths and weaknesses of the candidates as displayed by the interview, application forms, references and reports. This can be helpful and influential, but wise inspectors know how to leave the governors room to make the decision which is properly theirs.

Then there is the role of the head. If you have been a governor for some time you will know what weight to place upon the head's judgement. You will assist yourself here, however, if you have made a practice of following up past appointments in your visits to the school. Making appointments is not something that can be well done simply by turning up on the evening of the interview alone. Indeed, it causes understandable resentment among school staff if appointments are made by governors who have never seen the school during working hours.

Constraints are placed on questions governors may ask and comments they can make during discussion prior to decision. It is considered improper to question candidates about their politics or their religion (except for some positions in voluntary schools), although candidates may themselves volunteer information on both these topics. Race relations and equal opportunities legislation also make it illegal to allow either the race or the sex of a candidate to influence the decision.

The governors' decision after an appointment meeting is formally only a recommendation to the authority, but it is rare for such decisions to be overturned. There are two important respects in which effective decision-making is constrained, however. One is over the appointment of the head. Procedure for this differs from one authority to another, but in the majority of cases, the authority still reserves a major share of the final decision to itself, although there will almost certainly be involvement by the governors at some stage.

The other limitation on governors' freedom to choose staff is the provision in most articles that the authority may, if necessary, use the vacancy for placing a teacher on its staff who is displaced through reorganisation or some other cause. In years of falling rolls and school closures, contractions and amalgamations, this is a more widespread practice than heretofore. It is very important for governors to read the relevant clause in their articles very carefully indeed: there will probably be a requirement for the authority to consult with and listen to the views of the governing body before placing a teacher in this way. It would also be useful to try and get hold of a copy of the Staff Code for your authority. Although the articles may say that the authority *may* place a displaced teacher in a given vacancy, the Staff Code may not *compel* it to do so. (It may simply entitle the teacher to 'prior consideration'.) If the governors kick up enough fuss about what they feel is a totally unsuitable appointment being foisted on them, the authority may back down. On the other hand, it would be unfair and foolish to assume that all displaced teachers are inadequate: on the contrary you may pick up extremely valuable members of staff this way.

Chapter 9

Teachers – Establishment and Salaries

Establishment

The number of teachers that there are in school is a matter for the local education authority. There are minimum staffing standards that are set nationally; although before 1969 these laid down that no class in a secondary school should have more than 30 pupils, and no class in a primary school should have more than 40, since then the regulations have simply stated that each school should have a head teacher and a staff of assistant teachers 'suitable and sufficient in number'.

If the governors believe that the school has insufficient staff, they should make representations to the local authority. They may be helped in doing so by having some idea how their school compares with other schools in the authority's area, and how their authority compares with other authorities.

The simplest way of expressing the establishment of a school is by the teacher-pupil ratio. This is obtained by adding up all the teachers (with the exception of the head), and expressing this as a ratio of all the pupils. (Part-time teachers can be added up into 'full-time equivalents'; in other words four teachers working five half-days a week are two 'full-time equivalents'.) This figure is *not* the same as the normal class size of the school, nor even the average class size of the school (taking into account all the small teaching groups that are set up for various purposes). The teacher-pupil ratio is always better than the average class size, because there are always some teachers who are not teaching full-time, but have other responsibilities. Thus the fact that there are what you consider to be over-large classes in your school may not mean that you have an unfavourable pupil-teacher ratio. It may mean that there are a lot of very small teacher groups, or that a lot of teachers' time is being spent on something other than 'class contact' (things like writing timetables, seeing parents etc).

You should find out therefore what the teacher-pupil ratio of your school is, and how it compares with the authority's average for that type of school. (Secondary schools normally have better teacher-pupil ratios than primary schools.) If it is no worse than the average and yet you feel that the classes are bigger than classes at neighbouring schools, you should ask how the teachers are being deployed to reach this result. It may be that your school has very good reasons for needing *more* small teaching groups, or more time spent out of the classroom by teachers, than the normal school. If this is so, you should put these arguments as forcibly as you can to your local authority and appeal for more staff. On the other hand it may be that there is an unneccessary number of small groups being run (perhaps they are very small sixth-form groups that could well be taught together with those in a neighbouring school), or that too many staff are spending too much time not actually teaching. If so you should ask for a review of this situation.

If you want to know how the teacher-pupil ratio compares with that in other authorities, you can find these facts in the *Education Statistics* published annually by the Chartered Institute of Public Finance and Accountancy. Your local public library should be able to get hold of these documents for you.

The Training of Teachers

Hitherto teachers have become qualified in one of two ways. They have either taken a three-year (until 1960, a two-year) course of teacher training at a college of education, or they have taken a university degree, followed by one year of teacher training. Since 1974 all graduates entering teaching have had to have the year's training (except for scarce specialists in maths and science) and for some years all entrants to training have had to possess GCE O levels in English and maths.

In the last few years teacher training has been substantially reorganised. In the first place the colleges of education have been merged with polytechnics and other colleges. In the second place the numbers of teachers in training have been reduced because the demand for additional teachers has fallen. This means that teacher-training courses can choose among applicants and are increasingly accepting those who have the same qualifications as university entrants. In the third place, and connected with this, more teachers are taking an extra year and gaining a degree at the end of their professional training.

Salaries

The salaries of teachers are fixed nationally by a committee called the Burnham Committee, on which the teachers' organisations, the local authority associations and the Secretary of State are all represented. Teachers must, by law, be paid in accordance with the terms of the reports of this committee. The reports themselves, however, do allow local authorities a number of areas of discretion.

Looking at it from the teachers' point of view, the Burnham Reports provide for a number of salary scales, of which the first is a basic scale. A teacher who stays on this scale finds that his salary rises automatically (and on top of negotiated increases) each year until he reaches the top of the scale, when it stops rising. If the teacher is promoted he goes on to a higher scale, of which there are three – or he may become a deputy head or head.

Looking at it from the point of view of the school, what the Burnham Reports do is set out formulae for deciding how many of these promotion or 'scale' posts the school can offer. The formulae are based upon the numbers of pupils of various ages in the school. A pupil under 14 counts as two units, for example, and a 17-year-old pupil as eight units. The total of these units gives the number of 'points' that the school has. The Burnham Reports give schools of varying sizes a range of points, and the local authority can decide whether its schools are at the bottom, the middle or the top of the range. The Burnham Reports also allow additional points which the local authority may award for schools of exceptional difficulty.

Each of the various scales above the basic scale 'costs' a school a certain number of points – one point for scale 2, for example, and three points for scale 4. Clearly the school can 'spend' its points on any combination of posts carrying various scales of salary.

Remember that the Burnham Reports deal with the number of scale posts available – not with the total number of teachers there may be in the school. The latter is a matter of establishment.

The governors will certainly take an interest in the number of points the local authority says their school may have. It is open to them to put pressure on the local authority to move both their school and the other schools up the range which the Burnham Report allows. They can also apply to be considered as a school of exceptional difficulty.

When it comes to the distribution of the available points within the school, the head will make proposals for the governors to approve. This is not just a matter of seeing that the promotions are in some sense fair or sensible. The head will be using the salary scales to develop various aspects of the school's educational work. For example, he might concentrate higher scale posts in mathematics or crafts, because there are particular shortages of such teachers and he can use the extra money to attract applicants. He may reserve higher scale posts to offer to those members of staff who have pastoral or counselling responsibilities, because he believes this to be as important as subject specialisation. It is important when considering the distribution of scale posts to ask what are the *educational* consequences of the distribution.

It is good practice for the head to supply his governors from time to time with a list of all staff, with their responsibilities, and also a breakdown of the distribution of scale points between the various departments. If this does not happen, you should ask for it at an appropriate moment.

There are a number of other payments provided for in the Burnham Report, some of which allow for local discretion. There is an extra allowance for all teachers in the London area. There is an extra allowance on the lower scales for teachers with degrees. There is also an extra allowance for teachers working in schools of exceptional difficulty. (This is a payment to the *teachers*, and must be distinguished from the additional *points* given to the school for the same purpose.)

It is possible that during the next few years a new salary structure and conditions of service will be agreed by the Secretary of State, the local authorities and the teachers' associations.

Teachers' Strikes

For schools one of the most unhappy developments of recent years has been an increase in the number of occasions for dispute involving both teachers and non-teaching staff. Most schools have experienced some form of industrial 'action', including strikes. Governors will come to know that morale among school staffs is often low.

They will also realise that their own position is awkard. A dispute, especially about salaries, is between the teachers and their associations on the one hand and the employers (the local authorities) on the other. Yet the employers are also acting under the increasing influence of the Secretary of State. In these circumstances, what are the governors to do?

In the first place, it is not for them to get involved in the dispute – to which they are not parties. Their duty is to support the school in its difficulties through the exercise of their normal functions, for example through their concern for the conduct and curriculum of the school. Governors will almost certainly find that the head will report any days lost through strikes and any difficulties in maintaining normal operations through a withdrawal of 'goodwill'. Teacher governors will often be ready to explain what they and their colleagues are doing, both to further the dispute and to protect the interests of children.

The governors should make clear their interest in securing the continued and undisrupted education of children. The governors will recognise that they can secure this only through the head and staff. They need to understand why the teachers are striking and to recognise the external pressures on teachers and local authorities alike.

Governors may well disapprove of disruption and may think strikes an inappropriate weapon in schools, whatever the circumstances. Many teachers share these views. Others believe that disturbance now is necessary for future improvement or that there is simply no alternative to it. The difficult role for governors is to accept that the school is affected by a dispute over which they have no control and to try, calmly and with understanding, to discuss with the head and staff the ways in which as much as possible in the life of the school can be protected. It may not seem heroic at the time, but such a quiet, firm support is often effective in minimising damage and bitterness and laying the ground for better things when the dispute is over.

Chapter 10

Suspension of Pupils

It is often difficult for governors to know what they are supposed to do about suspension cases, and the law is not entirely helpful. The precise duties of governors in this respect are not specifically stated in the Education Acts and Regulations. However, a reference in the Pupils Registration Regulations 1956 to '. . . exclusion . . . by the Managers or Governors of the school' suggests that they have a responsibility in these cases.

The articles of government for every school *do* outline suspension procedures. They differ from authority to authority, but broadly speaking they give the head teacher the power to suspend a pupil but lay on him the obligation to report his action to the LEA and to the chairman of governors. A few authorities stipulate that parents should be informed that they have a right of appeal to the governors. This would imply that the governors do not merely receive the report from the head teacher but that they are required either to approve or refuse to approve the suspension, and to that extent they are a tribunal. Other articles are silent about what is expected of governors in these cases, but the general responsibility they are normally given for the 'conduct and curriculum' of the school could be held to cover arbitrating in cases of suspension.

A suspension is in theory only a temporary exclusion from school, though it can last a very long time. Once a pupil is permanently excluded, or expelled, his name is removed from the register of the school; until then it stays on the register, unless he is admitted to another school. During the period when a child is suspended, but not excluded, the possibility of his attending another school or being otherwise educationally provided for may or may not be explored. However, it remains the duty, throughout this period, of the LEA to provide education for him, and of his parents to see that he receives it.

The parents can appeal to the Secretary of State against the governor's confirmation of a suspension or exclusion (see page 70 in Chapter 16 on Public and Private Pressures).

The practice relating to the consideration of suspension varies widely; it can consist of the barest reporting, with no discussion, or it can be a lengthy 'hearing' with the parents present. You may feel dissatisfied with the way suspensions are handled by your governing body. It would be hard for an individual governor to initiate a completely new procedure, like the one outlined at the end of this section, in one school, and if you feel the procedure needs revising this is a case for a resolution (or a paper) to the local authority. There are, however, ways in which a governor can improve the situation short of this.

First, you can relate what is happening in this case to the system of discipline generally. When you are faced with a suspension case you need background information of the sort you can only really have gained by visiting the school regularly. This is one of those cases where just turning up for the meeting will not do. The sort of things you will have to know about in advance in order to deal with a suspension intelligently are answers to these questions: Who in the school is responsible for the welfare of each individual pupil (what is often referred to as the 'pastoral system')? What is the system of dealing with disruptive children? What are the sanctions against bad behaviour? At what stage are parents involved in cases of bad behaviour? What use is made of the Educational Welfare Service, or other relevant agency? You will probably get from the answers to these questions a notion of whether or not the school is positively seeking to take 'avoiding action' before a situation reaches suspension.

Second, when a suspension is reported at a governors' meeting you should certainly make sure that the parents and other agencies have been involved in the case; and you can ask what their views on the situation are. There may be reports from the educational psychologist or social worker which are relevant to your decision and should be available to the governing body. You should also make sure that the chairman has been consulted. In most articles of government the headmaster is obliged to report a suspension to the chairman, if not the whole body of governors, and so he at any rate should have a full picture of what is happening. If you are not happy about a particular case, or about suspension practice in your school generally, you can ask to discuss it privately with the chairman.

Third, if your authority is one in which the parents are told that they have the right of appeal, and if you are involved in a case where the parents do actually appear before the governors, it is important to make the parents feel that you have not pre-judged the issue, and to give them as much opportunity as possible to put their point of view. Some articles may allow for the parent to bring a friend (who may or may not be a legal adviser). If this is not in your articles, but you feel that it would be fairer, you can suggest it to the chairman in advance.

Fourth, you should certainly ask as part of any consideration of a suspension, what educational provision is being made for the child. This is always a headache for the local authority's officers as it is not always easy to place a child who has been suspended, and special units for disruptive or disturbed children may have long waiting lists. The officer present at the meeting may in fact be glad of an opportunity to explain the difficulties a suspension puts him in. Some officers, like some ordinary members of the public, think that a minority of head teachers use suspension too freely as a way of getting rid of their problems and a good head, in their eyes, is one who rarely suspends. Consequently, asking what education the suspended child is to receive serves the dual purpose of checking up that some provision is being made, even if it is only a few hours a week of home tuition, and of making it clear to all present that the problem of this particular child does not end with his suspension.

Some authorities prepare leaflets about local provision for disturbed children, truancy centres, available psychiatric advice, and so on. This would in any case be of interest to governors, but may be particularly relevant to the consideration of cases of suspension. You could ask the clerk if such a document is available, and if it is not, suggest that it be prepared and circulated.

A suspension case may sometimes give rise to issues concerning the conduct of the school that governors feel need discussing outside the context of this particular case – questions to do with uniform rules, corporal punishment, playground supervision and so on. If this is the case, when the suspension case is finished, but before the meeting rises, you should express your concern and ask that an item to discuss it (or to ask the headmaster to report on it) be put on the agenda for the next meeting. If it is sufficiently serious and urgent you can ask for a special meeting, but check in your articles how many governors have to ask for it (usually it is two).

The Government has recently made new proposals on suspension proceedings (see page 89) but while responsibility for confirming or reversing suspensions still rests with the governing body, readers may find the following suggested procedures put forward by the National Association of Governors and Managers interesting:

NAGM's Recommendations:

Emergency Procedures

1. The head of the school should have certain powers for instant suspension of a pupil, to be used only when he feels that the interests of other pupils demand this action. If he invokes these powers, he should immediately inform/consult the parent and in any event within 24 hours inform the parent, the chairman of governors and the LEA.
2. For short periods of suspension, ie up to 10 days, the head should have the right to suspend a pupil. There should be no need to call an emergency meeting of governors. However, he must report everything that has happened to the next convenient meeting of governors and, of course, keep the chairman and the LEA informed at the time.
3. However, if he wishes to continue the suspension of a pupil beyond 10 days, or for any other reason wishes this temporary suspension to be considered by the governors, an emergency meeting of the governors must be called as soon as possible, and not later than 14 days from the original date of suspension.

Normal Suspension Procedures

4. In all other than emergency cases, if the head is considering the question of suspending a pupil, he must inform the parent and give him or her up to seven days to discuss the situation.
5. He should simultaneously inform the LEA and chairman of governors and invite reactions and comments from them.
6. He should seek the LEA's assistance in summoning an emergency case conference at the school of all who have been concerned with the child – educational psychologist, class teacher, social worker, juvenile bureau, etc – to discuss the situation, within 10 days.
7. If, after this period of time has elapsed, he still then wishes to go ahead with a full consideration of suspension, an emergency meeting of the governors should be called within 21 days of the original

notification to the parents and, if possible, these procedures should be gone through whilst the pupil is still attending school.

Representations and Advice for Parents and Pupil Concerned

8. It should be open to the parent/pupil to bring a 'friend' to any proceedings to consider the suspension. A friend should be anyone the parent/pupil wishes to bring to help them present their case.

9. As part of the procedure before a hearing of suspension before the governors, it should be the duty of the LEA to advise the parent/pupil on all aspects of the proposed suspension, and of their rights in relation to the suspension procedure, including their right of appeal against the governors' decision to the Secretary of State under Section 68. The LEA should make available an officer who shall have the duty of advising the parents/pupil in these matters, and such an officer should be one who is not involved in any way in the proceedings on behalf of any of the other parties. It should also be the LEA's duty to advise parents of other voluntary/statutory agencies who may be able to help the parents/pupil with the situation arising from the possible suspension.

Proceedings before the Governors on the Question of Suspension

10. The object of the procedure is to combine fairness with speed. The governors, although they have semi-judicial functions, are not a court of law, and the emphasis should be not so much on the hearing of conflicting 'cases', as on agreement as to what happened and what should be done.

11. All concerned parties should be present. It should be the duty of the chairman to explain the form the proceedings should take.

12. The head and staff involved should first explain the problem as they see it, and, if they wish, make recommendations to the governors.

13. The officer of the LEA should then present additional information from reports submitted by other agencies (see 6).

14. The parent/pupil/friend should then be given the opportunity to ask questions or challenge anything that has been said.

15. The parent/pupil/friend should then explain the situation as they see it and make any recommendations that they want to.

16. The head and staff involved should then ask any questions that they may wish.

17. The governors should have the right to intervene and ask questions where appropriate.

18. The parent/pupil/friend and the head and any staff involved (but not the staff governor if he is not personally involved) should then retire while the governors then consider whether or not they will suspend.

19. If the governors decide to suspend they shall either
    (a) suspend for a limited period after which the child shall be re-admitted to school, or
    (b) recommend that the child be excluded from school and that the LEA make alternative educational provision for him.

20.　On no account should a child be suspended for more than eight weeks.

21.　It should be the duty of the governors to enquire of the LEA what provision it is making for the care and education of the child who is suspended.

Chapter 11

Staff Discipline

There is a commonly held belief that it is impossible to dismiss a teacher. This is not true. What is true is that fairly serious allegations have to be made and substantiated in order for action to be taken. These allegations would generally have to be of misconduct or indiscipline, but can also include incompetence – though the proving of this is not easy.

There will probably be a reference to the procedure to be followed in cases of complaint against teachers in your articles. If there is not, or if the provisions are not clear, you can ask your Director of Education or Chief Education Officer if you could see a copy of the Staff Code for teachers in your authority. This is probably a document that has been agreed with the teachers' unions and may lay down a detailed procedure for the hearing of complaints and the action that can be taken after the finding of these hearings: such action may include dismissal, downgrading and reprimand.

Since teachers are employed and paid by the authority, it is the authority that takes the final decision in disciplinary matters. (The teacher can, of course, then appeal to the Industrial Tribunal.) The governors may or may not be involved in a case before it reaches the authority for final decision. This depends very much on the articles and Staff Code in each authority and the way in which the complaint has arisen. Many complaints will go direct to the education officer, either from the head, from a parent or from another teacher.

In a voluntary school it is more likely that the governors will be involved, since although the authority pays the salary of teachers, the teachers are actually employed by the governors or managers. Even here, however, the authority will have a final say of some sort in the matter.

If a complaint does come to the governors it is important that you know what the proper procedure is. Make sure you have a senior officer of the authority present to advise you, both on how to proceed and what courses of action are open to you. A special meeting should be arranged for the hearing of the complaint, and the teacher has the right to appear before the governing or managing body with a 'friend', which usually means a lawyer or a union adviser. The governors do not have their own legal adviser (some people feel that in cases of this sort they should be allowed one) and it is therefore all the more important that you should get proper advice, including legal advice, from the authority.

One thing it is important to know is how and whether the governing body can initiate proceedings. This is clearly a very serious step, and you would hope not to have to take it, but there are rare occasions when it is the right and necessary thing to do. The Auld Report on William Tyndale School, it is worth remembering, suggested that this was an action the managers in that case should have considered.

There are several obvious reasons why a governing body would be loath to invite complaints against a teacher. It takes a degree of courage to say what has to be said in a formal meeting. Also, people are often frightened of getting involved in litigation themselves, though this is unlikely if you are sure of your facts and have evidence to back your complaints. What you say in a governors' meeting is governed by the rules of 'qualified privilege' – that is, you cannot be sued for slander unless it can be shown that you were actuated by 'malice'. It is of the utmost importance to observe the strictest confidentiality about disciplinary proceedings of any kind.

In this chapter we should also mention another possible situation that might arise. Most articles make special provision for the right of communication from the staff to the governors, and some staff may use this clause to put individual grievances to the governors. (Matters on which there is strong feeling on the part of a lot of the staff are more likely to come through the teacher governor.) Such communications must be dealt with seriously, courteously and impartially. If there is friction in the staffroom the governors will do no one any good by starting off with the presumption that the head is always right – or wrong.

Chapter 12

Conduct and Curriculum

Somewhere in your articles there will be a reference to your responsibilities as a governor over either 'conduct' or 'curriculum' or, more usually, both. It is important to be familiar with the passage and the exact form of words, so that you will be confident in justifying your questions about how the school is run and what it is teaching, at governors' meetings. However, you may think the words do not make it very clear what you are supposed to do. Usually they do not. They give governors a very vaguely defined 'overseeing' or 'directing' function, while leaving the head teacher with 'day-to-day' and 'internal' matters. Almost any issue of importance in a school – whether or not to introduce mixed-ability teaching, or abolish corporal punishment, for instance – could be described as coming under either category of functions, and it is therefore almost impossible for you as a governor to tell how far your writ runs. The Taylor Report suggested a completely new definition of the governors' responsibilities in this matter (see page 79), and the Government made its own proposals in 1985 (see page 89).

Meanwhile, the best guidance is to reflect on the basic purpose of having a governing body of ordinary non-professional people at all. You are not there to keep a detailed check on the professional work of the school. That is the job of the local authority's inspectors and advisers, who should visit the school regularly and be available to discuss the curriculum or any aspect of it with the governors. The governors are there to make sure that the head and staff have a regular opportunity, indeed obligation, to give an account in plain terms of what they are doing and what they are hoping to achieve, and to gain the support of the governors for their activities. The governors can defend educational standards in their school not by laying down what they should be, but by seeing that the school itself has some.

Do not allow yourself to be silenced by jargon and statistics. The educational world is fuller than most of mystifying terminology and initials: some are useful shorthand for those who use them often, but some are unnecessary. Always ask for terms you do not understand to be expalined. Similarly, do not assume that statistics of exam entries and passes and attendance rates can give you a complete profile of a school. The reality of life and work in a school is a complex thing, and probably no one person has a complete view of it. Your view, as a concerned non-professional outsider, is one part of the picture and important in its own right. Any sensible head will take serious note of it.

However, he will probably do so only if you are reasonably familiar with the school and are in the habit of visiting it. Chapter 15 goes into the practicalities of visiting. What should be said here in connection with your overall responsibilities for the 'conduct and curriculum' of the school is that the best way of evaluating what you see when you visit is by going back to fundamentals. Schools are after all about young children and young people learning, and it is by looking at *them* that you will have some clue about the success of the school. Do the children look happy and as if they know what they are doing? Are they concentrating and showing signs of interest? If the answer to these questions is 'no', then whatever the duplicated sheets about the curriculum say and however impressive it sounds, there are shortcomings somewhere in it all.

There is just one word of warning. In this area above all, it is of prime importance to remember that your power as a governor does not belong to you individually, but only as a member of the whole corporate body. It is wrong for an individual governor to try to make the head, or worse any particular member of staff, adopt a particular policy. Such action is only properly exercised by the governing body as a whole, by discussion and if necessary by formal resolution in a properly convened meeting.

Other chapters, particularly those on the head's report and suspensions, give examples of how governors can raise issues of conduct and curriculum at governors' meetings. Appointment meetings are also important occasions for discussing the curricular aims of the school. In general the best method is to use any opportunity possible to express interest and ask questions on specific issues, rather than to stake out your formal claims to responsibility in these matters. However, this chapter tries to clarify what those claims could be, should the need arise.

Special Educational Needs

Under the Education Act, 1981, governors have a specific responsibility towards children with special educational needs, that is those with greater difficulties in learning than most of their contemporaries or those with particular disabilities. The governors must try to see that if any pupil in the school has special educational needs then special educational provision is made, that the needs of such children are made known to all who teach them and that teachers in the school understand the importance of identifying and providing for such pupils.

Governors visiting the school can ask how many pupils have special educational needs and what is being done for them. At governors' meetings, a convenient occasion for discussing this will no doubt be the head's report. Many schools are just getting used to the new responsibilities placed upon them by the 1981 Act and you will almost certainly find the head and staff ready to discuss their problems and the steps they are taking to solve them.

The role of governors of special schools is further discussed in Chapter 19.

New Developments

The last five years have seen a significant increase in the number of initiatives affecting the curriculum which have been taken by central government. The Secretary of State has sought to influence, even to control, what happens in schools through pressure on local authorities on the content of the curriculum and through reform to the system of public examinations. The Manpower Services Commission has also exercised pressure through additional funding for its Technical and Vocational Education Initiative. Governors will want to know what has been the effect of these pressures and intitiatives on the work of their own schools.

One of the Secretary of State's initiatives, however, may involve governors more directly. The Secretary of State is directly funding a number of pilot schemes to develop records of achievement. The object of this is to find ways in which all young people in secondary schools will have a record of what they have done in school when they leave.

A small number of schools and authorities have decided to tackle the problem of giving national currency to records of achievement. A pilot scheme, funded by the Gulbenkian Foundation, is testing a framework in which the courses which young people take up at the 'options' stage two years before the end of compulsory education, are 'validated' by a body established for this purpose by the governors of the school. The records, when produced two years later, are 'accredited' by a body set up by the local authority. And this accreditation is given national currency by a pilot national body which the participating authorities have combined to establish. What the participating schools have already discovered is that the activity of validation greatly enhances governors' responsibility for the conduct and curriculum of the school. (See *Records of Achievement at Sixteen,* Tyrrell Burgess and Elizabeth Adams, NFER-Nelson, 1985.)

Chapter 13

Admissions

In county schools, the system of admission of children to school is controlled by the local education authority, although some articles of government require that the head and governors be consulted. In voluntary schools, the gobvernors are responsible for admissions, as long as they act in accordance with arrangements agreed with the local authority. In practice this means that the head teacher of a voluntary school has a lot more discretion over which children he admits (though answerable to his governors) than does the head of a county school who is given guidelines by the local authority if he handles admissions at all.

Controlling both county and voluntary school admissions is the law, which states (Schools Regulations 1959): 'A pupil shall not be refused admission to or excluded from a school on other than reasonable grounds'; and also (1944 Act, Section 76): 'Local education authorities shall have regard to the general principle that, so far as is compatible with the provision of efficient instruction and training and the avoidance of unreasonable public expenditure, pupils are to be educated in accordance with the wishes of their parents'.

In the past these general provisions of the law seemed to conflict with the local authority's wish to make rational and efficient use of all its schools: it would want to ensure that no school was overcrowded and no school unreasonably empty. A long-standing policy to reduce the size of classes, for example, would be threatened if popular schools became overfull. In the past parents who were denied their preference for a school could only appeal to the Secretary of State that the local authority was acting unreasonably (1944 Act, Section 68) and was thus neglecting the general principle that pupils should be educated in accordance with the wishes of their parents (Section 76).

In the 1970s the number of appeals to the Secretary of State increased, for two reasons. The first was that with the abolition of selection at 11, parents had more choice of secondary schools to which their children might go and came to feel that the choice was more important. Second, a decline in the numbers of school age children, though itself increasing the possibility of choice, did also increase the chance that some schools would become so small as to be inefficient and uneconomic. The Education Act, 1980, dealt with these problems by making new legal arrangements for parental preference.

The Act requires every local education authority to enable a parent to express a preference for a school which he wishes his child to attend and to give reasons for the preference. The local authority and the governors of county and voluntary schools must comply with this preference unless this 'would prejudice the provision of efficient education or the efficient use of resources';

or if it were incompatible with the arrangments made by the authority with an aided or special agreement school; or if it conflicted with admission by selection according to ability or aptitude.

Local authorities also have to make arrangements to enable parents to appeal against a refusal by the authority or by the governors to admit a child to a preferred school. The arrangments for appeal in aided or special agreement are made by the governors. The decisions of appeals committees are binding on the local authority and the governors.

Local authorities and the governors of aided and special agreement schools must publish annually information on the arrangements for admission and for appeal. The information must include the number of pupils to be admitted in each school year, the admission functions of the local authority and the governors and the policy followed in deciding admissions.

These new arrangements have somewhat reduced the involvement of governors in admissions. Nevertheless it is their duty to be perfectly clear about what the authority's admission system, both to primary and to secondary schools, is. What is the maximum number of children to be admitted, who has priority, who is actually to say yes or no to the parents applying? Are places to be left open for latecomers to the area, and if so how many? Is there a 'catchment area'? If so, what grounds for exceptional admission are there? When the governors are clear about the system run by their local authority, they should then ensure, first, that it is in fact being carried out, and second that the information made available is clear. If there is a catchment area, it should be publicly displayed. If there is a system of priority of admission to oversubscribed schools, it should be publicly stated. Nothing causes more ill-will against a school, and its head teacher, than a suspicion that an unfair and capricious system of selection is at work, and it is an important function of the governors to ensure that their school does not have this reputation. It is particularly easily acquired by a voluntary school, where admission is still usually subject to interview of parents and child. If you are the governor or manager of a voluntary school, the responsibility for admissions rests on you though it may by tradition be wholly delegated to the head teacher. It is therefore particularly your duty to make sure that the head teacher is operating the system fairly and according to known criteria.

If you are a governor of a county school and you feel that the arrangements for admission are not working well, you should make representations to the local authority about it. You may be asked for your views, and if you are not you should offer them in any case. You may want to advise on a change of the catchment area, or a different linking of local schools. Although the authority has responsibility for the pattern overall, you, as members of the local community, are in a unique position to see how it is actually working out 'on the ground', and the authority should be grateful for this sort of information.

You may occasionally be approached as a governor by parents who have been refused admission for their child at your school. They may feel that you have some special 'pull' with the head teacher or officers. This puts you in an awkward position: on the one hand you want to help a disappointed individual, but on the other hand you do not want to be a party to queue jumping through private connections. What you can do is, first, to check that the parents were refused admission for valid reasons in terms of the system being operated:

it is after all possible that there was an error. Next you can explain the system to the parents and tell them how they should properly appeal, if they do not already know. If you feel particularly strongly about the case you can ask for it to be discussed at the governors' meeting. What you should not do is try to use you position as a governor or manager to get special treatment for a case that has no particular merit except that it is known to you. This probably will not work (or should not work) and causes resentment all round.

Chapter 14

Reorganisation and Closure

Almost all local education authorities are involved in school reorganisations of some sort. There are a number of reasons for this:

1. The rapid fall in the birth rate between 1965 and 1980 has meant falling school rolls and has raised questions over the viability of some schools. (The birth rate has since risen slightly, but not yet nearly enough to return to the previous levels);

2. There has been an even more rapid depopulation of some village and inner city areas;

3. More young people are staying in education after 16, to do a greater variety of courses;

4. In the nature of things, buildings outlive their useful life and may be too costly to maintain or replace;

5. Closing schools may save money;

6. In some authorities, school sites are coveted for other purposes (eg, private development).

The problems are different in different sorts of schools and different sorts of areas. What would be regarded as a school too small to be viable in a city may be the only sensible solution in a rural area. Also, in some parts of the country it is the rural areas that are deprived and need extra support; in others they are relatively privileged, and it would be more equitable for extra resources to be concentrated on the more built-up areas. Reorganisation proposals will always be judged by their effect on the area as a whole, not just the individual village or neighbourhood. The duty of the governor is to hold in balance the interests of the community as a whole, and those of the particular school. It is his duty to see that the latter are properly articulated.

The Stages of Closure or Reorganisation

There are four stages in any reorganisation plan: the private deliberations within the LEA; the public consultation; the decision by the council, the publication of notices and the appeal to the Secretary of State; and the implementation of the agreed plan.

The Private Deliberations

A responsible LEA will be keeping the size and distribution of its schools under constant review, and may from time to time decide that some changes are needed. It is at this point – where the LEA decides something must be done – that the consultation procedure should be initiated. If the LEA goes on to decide behind closed doors what the change ought to be, this is contrary to the principle of open government. If you get wind of any secret discussions about closing a school, it is perfectly fair to protest and, if necessary, to make a public fuss.

The Public Consultation

All consultation exercises should start with an open mind. We set out below the practice adopted by the ILEA: it is not necessarily the best (though it has been officially commended by HMI), but it is an example of what is possible and can be used as a contrast to less open procedures.

1. The LEA should start by laying the problem before a meeting of heads and governors (including teacher and parent governors) in the area affected. This 'facts and figures' paper should contain:
   - existing roll numbers for each school, with numbers for each year group;
   - present and predicted demographic change, including flows in and out of the area;
   - transport patterns in the area;
   - other users, and other potential users, of the buildings.

2. Once these data have been presented and digested, say two weeks later, the education officer (not at this stage the councillors) should put forward a number of different options (see the following section on primary and secondary forms of organisation), and invite other suggestions from the community. The education officer's paper should describe all the possible forms of organisation that are in operation elsewhere in the country, so that the public does not feel constrained to stick with the existing pattern of organisation.

3. After a period of several months for meetings, discussions and other forms of consultation, the education committee should consider all the options submitted, and, with the advice of its officers, make a decision, publicly.

The LEA's Decision and the Publication of Notices

The law is that:

1. For a county school, only the LEA can publish a proposal for change, whether it is closure, amalgamation or the establishment of a new school.

2. The LEA must publish a notice and allow a specified time for appeals. Ask your clerk for a clear note of the law. All such proposals are subject to the approval of the Secretary of State. If you want to lodge an appeal, make sure you know the closing date. Appeals are seriously considered and can sometimes be successful: it is therefore well worth while mobilising opinion against a proposal you feel to be wrong.

3. In the case of a voluntary school, only the governors can propose a change in character (age group, single-sex or mixed, selective or

comprehensive), but the LEA can propose closure of a voluntary school.

Implementation

This is the most often neglected part of the process. Once the decisions have been approved, media interest dies and local campaigners give up. However, schools are particularly at risk during this period, both those that are closing and those that are changing in some way. Often promises have been made during the consultation period – for more staff, or extra facilities, or guaranteed access for particular groups of children – which the LEA is then half-hearted about honouring. It is important to keep all the committee papers in relation to the reorganisation for future reference, in order to make sure that promises are fulfilled.

How to Judge a Reorganisation Proposal

There are three sorts of consideration to bear in mind – educational, social and financial.

Educational Considerations – Primary Schools

Most LEAs will start considering the possibility of closure if a primary school roll looks like dropping much below 100 (in a built-up area) or 60 (in a rural area). There are two educational problems associated with small schools:

1. The difficulty of teaching mixed-age classes.
2. The narrow range of teaching skills/specialisms in a school with only two or three teachers.

Against this, it has to be stated that the quality of teaching in some small village primary schools is excellent.

Possible Different Ways of Organising Small Primary Schools

1. Peripatetic specialist teachers working between a group of small primary schools, to enrich the curriculum.
2. The organisation of groups of small primary schools in clusters, perhaps even federated under one head, so that teaching expertise can be shared.
3. The preservation of infant and nursery (three to seven) schools in the villages, with transfer at seven to a combined Junior School.

Educational Considerations – Secondary Schools

The 'accepted wisdom' about secondary education is that a comprehensive school, even without a sixth form, is not viable if it goes much below five-form entry (150 pupils in a year). In some rural areas it will perforce be much smaller than this, and even in city areas there are some exceptional four- or even three-form entry comprehensive schools which flourish. The educational arguments against allowing a proliferation of small comprehensive schools are as follows:

1. A secondary curriculum demands a range of specialist staff: a staff below 35 in number may not be sufficiently varied and diverse in its expertise to provide the necessary 'spark' to all its members: at a 1 to 15 ratio, which is generous, a three-form entry school would fall below this.
2. Small schools cannot offer a range of curricular options. Against this, there are in fact many successful small schools, and governors may feel that the particular circumstances of their schools make it one of these.

Educational Considerations: Education Over 16

Where there is a problem of sixth forms becoming too small (and this is increasingly the case), the education authority should be looking at its provision for all its 16–19 year-olds – including its further education colleges. Schools cannot be considered in isolation from this age group.

Social Considerations of School Closure and Reorganisation

Often the main argument for preserving a small school is that it is the most important, and perhaps the only, focus for community life. This should not be a reason for preserving a school that is not viable on educational grounds; but it should be an argument for the building to be retained for community/educational use. Governors who are close to the local community should be in a strong position to argue for a viable alternative use.

Financial Considerations of School Closure

LEAs will be reluctant to admit a financial motive for wanting to close schools, but they should be pressed closely about the projected savings and their proposals for the site and buildings of any school to be closed. It is perfectly proper to consider the financial implications, but it should be done openly and in the context of the council's total budget. This means, for instance, that the total costs of public services in a village should be borne in mind when decisions are being taken that a village school is 'uneconomic'. It is possible that, although the teacher-pupil ratios have to be very favourable, the other costs of maintaining the school are very low, and the village is short of other services such as buses.

Some Other Points in Relation to a School Closure or Reorganisation

Closure or amalgamation? The detailed proposals of any scheme deserve careful scrutiny. Amalgamation is often proposed as an easier option than closure. It may be preferable for the following reasons:

1. Staff from both schools are treated equally. (Technically, when there is an amalgamation both schools 'close', and the new school opens. All staff apply, on equal terms, for the jobs in the new school.)
2. Consequently there is not one 'dying' school, where staff are leaving as soon as they can find other jobs. The building which is gradually being closed is staffed by teachers appointed to the 'new' school.

Avoiding Disruption

Parents and teachers in a school that is to be closed or reorganised should seek guarantees about the rate at which the school is to be run down. Children should not be expected to move more than once during their secondary school career, and not in the middle of an examination course.

New Building

Capital building controls imposed by the Government have been tightening in recent years, and it would be unrealistic in most counties to propose reorganisations that involved major rebuilding (unless you have a really hard roofs-over-heads argument). This is particularly important if you are proposing a 'tertiary college' scheme. It will probably involve closing/amalgamating a secondary school in order to release the necessary accommodation. The further education college is probably overcrowded as it is.

What Governors Can Do

This chapter has described the various processes that have to be gone through in relation to the closure or change of character of a school, and the sorts of arguments that are likely to be deployed during the consultations. The governors' role is fourfold. First, they have a duty to make sure that the proposals are as widely and fairly discussed as possible. Certain statutory duties to consult are laid on the local education authority, but these are the statutory minimum; governors, from their knowledge of staff, parents and the local community, should be able to suggest the most convenient and appropriate sorts of meeting.

Second, if they are sure the local authority's plans for the school are wrong, and will be damaging, they should publicly identify themselves with the campaign against them by participating as fully as possible.

But third, when and if this battle is lost, they should concentrate all their efforts on getting the best possible deal for the children and staff of the school. The stage at which the second sort of activity turns into the third is a matter of judgement, but it is the third stage where the governors' support, concentration on detailed organisation and energetic lobbying of councillors may be the most important.

Fourth, where the school continues through reorganisation the governors should support the school in the inevitable difficulties, seeking help as required from the LEA, and should in particular be alerted to see that promises made to the school are not, in the event, broken.

Chapter 15

Visiting the School

You need to visit the school of which you are a governor first to find out how you can help the school, second to help yourself to understand what the school is doing, third to be supportive to the head teacher in his need to have a concerned outsider with whom to discuss problems, and fourth – and this is a specific duty laid on you by the articles – to inspect the fabric of the buildings and report on them to the authority.

If you are a parent of a child at the school, it is probably relatively easy to find occasions to visit the school regularly and informally, particularly if it is a school that encourages parents to involve themselves in the life of the school. Even if you are not a parent, schools of this sort will probably be glad of extra help, if you have the time to do this. You could offer, for instance, to accompany a class outing or to help with some particular club activity. Even if you only do this once or twice it will give you an opportunity to get some feel of how the school functions and what its needs and problems are.

If the school does not provide this sort of opportunity readily or if you do not feel up to it yourself, there is still a lot that can be achieved by a simple visit, or by a succession of visits. The object should be to get to know the head and staff sufficiently well so that they will regard your visits as opportunities to discuss some of the school's problems, rather than as disruptive 'red carpet' occasions. Of course, you should always make an appointment, unless you are genuinely on such intimate terms with the school that the head will have no compunction about asking you to come another time, if inconvenient.

Both you and the head teacher will be less at a loss if you make some pretext for coming to the school – that you want, for instance, to see how a new building is functioning, or what improvements should be urged on the authority in respect of some of the accommodation. Or you can express an interest in some curricular development the head has mentioned at a governors' meeting and ask if you could learn more about it from the teacher concerned. Once you are there, however, you should be ready to be distracted by anything else the head wants to draw your attention to: the visit is a good opportunity to check up on the development of matters that have been raised at meetings, to find out how staff recently appointed are getting on, and whether difficulties with other agencies have been sorted out. If the head realises that your concern extends beyond the few hours of the governors' meeting, you may find he is very ready to confide in you – the more so if you follow up your enquiries with action, either at the meetings, or (through the chairman) outside them, or informally, like knowing of a possible flat for a new teacher who has a long journey.

If you are in the habit of making frequent brief visits to the school it will be easier to approach the head about any subject that is worrying you. Parents and others may approach you from time to time with complaints. You should always try first to persuade them to go direct to the head. If they will not, then it is your duty to take their complaints seriously and pursue them with the head. It is not a good idea to take up a complaint with the head for the first time at a governors' meeting. He is then forced into a defensive posture, whereas if you mention it privately to him, he may be grateful for the information and set about putting the matter right. However, if the head refuses to listen to what you feel is a justified complaint, and the matter is sufficiently serious, you may feel you have no alternative but to bring it to the attention of the chairman, or raise it at a governors' meeting. As you get to know the rest of the staff, too, you may feel able to take up complaints or disturbing rumours with them, though as a general rule it is better to communicate first with the head.

When you visit, the head teacher will probably take you into classrooms, but some heads and teachers still feel that this is an intrusion. You must try and overcome this reluctance with friendly persistence: it is self-evident that it is difficult to 'oversee' the education of the school unless you can see it where it is happening. Nevertheless, your 'right' of access to classrooms depends on a decision by the governing body as a whole that you should have it. If the head does not want you to visit classrooms you cannot argue it out with him individually. It should be discussed and resolved upon by the governing body as a whole, which should also, if there is any uneasiness about the subject, establish procedures for making appointments, giving individual classroom teachers notice, and so on. These should then be scrupulously adhered to.

Different governors – like anyone else – look for different things in a school, depending on their interests and their view of what is important and significant. Some governors swear that you can tell more about the morale of a school by looking at the state of the lavatories than by anything else, others concentrate on the staffroom or the atmosphere in the corridors at lesson changing time. A check on all these things (not necessarily in the same visit) as on such things as provision for remedial teaching, the library, sixth-form accommodation, specialist provision, should be made by some governor or other during the course of the year, and it is sensible for governors to check up either formally or informally with each other to make sure most areas are covered.

Whatever you are going ostensibly to see, however, at the back of your mind can be two questions which may be of some guidance: has this school got what it needs? (Is the authority making adequate provision?) Is it doing what it should be doing? (Are the children learning?) The first of these questions is the easier to deal with, and the sort of investigation and action needed have been discussed in the chapters on finance, accommodation and establishment. The other is far harder, and it is, of course, the one which a good head and staff will be asking themselves all the time. It can certainly not be answered by the visiting governor in any complete way, only – in some form or other – asked. There is discussion of this in Chapter 12 on Conduct and Curriculum.

Chapter 16

Public and Private Pressures

Pressure Within the School

Chapter 15 on Visiting the School has already described the ways in which a governor can, by showing his serious concern for the school, establish a relationship in which it is possible to offer suggestions for improvement. No profession takes kindly to criticism from amateurs, and teachers are probably as defensive as most; for this reason you will probably find that a diffidently expressed worry may establish a better atmosphere in which to pursue what you see as a shortcoming then a blunt expression of opinion.

If you feel that something may be going seriously wrong in a school -- whether it is the discipline, the relations with parents or whatever else – you should make an appointment to discuss it with the head. It is a useful discipline, particularly if you are feeling agitated or heated about the subject yourself, to envisage for a moment or two before you start the sort of pressures under which most head teachers operate. He is probably conscious of a pile of urgent matters, involving the welfare of the teachers and pupils for whom he is responsible, requiring action and decision and personal intervention from him; and although it is right that he should make time for you he may very well be hoping that your visit will not last very long and will not involve anything that adds to his burdens. For this reason you should not regard an immediate defensive reaction to your request as necessarily his final thought on the subject. He may very well, when he has time to give it some thought, and if you make it clear that this is all you want him to do initially, come to a different view and try to effect some improvement.

Another possible reaction from a head teacher, if your worry is something like academic standards in particular subjects, is to admit the problem, but feel unable for a variety of reasons to solve it. What you can do here is suggest ways in which the governors might support him in his attempt to reach a solution – by getting extra staff or help from the inspectorate for a weak department for instance, or by asking for more information at a governors' meeting, so as to oblige the department concerned to put in some thought about their work. If you feel you are getting nowhere at all through talking to the head, then you should approach the chairman of governors and ask for his advice and help. He may suggest that you should raise the matter at a governors' meeting or take some other action. If you are not satisfied with his answer, and even if he discourages you from raising it at a governors' meeting, you can still do so if you feel the matter is sufficiently urgent. (See Chapter 4 on The Agenda.)

You can also, or you can ask you chairman to, approach the officers of the authority, or your local councillor or education committee member. There is a danger here of appearing to go behind the back of the head and the other governors, and it is well to have the structure of the William Tyndale Report in mind, and try to have the whole matter discussed openly at a governors' meeting. Mr Auld's advice, reprinted below, applies when there is a very serious rift between the head and some governors, and it is obviously a difficult personal judgement at what stage your discussions become sufficiently serious to affect the jobs of individuals and the future of the school, and therefore must in justice not be discussed confidentially with officers and members without the knowledge of the head and chairman. Any matter you take up without the authorisation of the governing body you are, of course, doing informally and as an individual.

Extract from the Auld Report

834. However, if the managers and the head teacher disagree about the managers' anxiety, or relations between them generally are bad, then a number of considerations have to be taken into account. They are as follows:

(i) The managers should act corporately. This is particularly important now that the head teacher and one of his staff are members of the managing body. Whatever the managers decide to do, they should decide together, and by vote if necessary, at a properly constituted managers' meeting. There should be no decisions taken by factions of the managing body. Nor should there be meetings between members of the managing body with the Authority's representatives to discuss the problem in the absence and without the knowledge of the chairman of the managers, or of the head teacher or the teacher-manager.

(ii) Managerial oversight can only be exercised under Rule 2 of the Rules of Management in consultation with the head teacher. If he disagrees with the managers on a point of importance relating to the conduct and curriculum of the school, it would be wrong, and totally counter-productive, for the managers, to force their 'oversight' upon the school in the form of managerial visits which are really lay 'inspections'. Such visits would be wrong whether decided upon collectively and by vote at a managers' meeting or individually by certain managers. Pending the action to which I refer in the next sub-paragraph, managers should be sparing in the managerial visits they make. They should also be scrupulous to visit only by appointment and to avoid, so far as possible, any behaviour of an 'inspectorial' nature. I use the words, 'so far as possible', because I appreciate that the dividing line between a managerial visit and an 'inspectorial' visit by a critical manager may not always be easy to draw.

(iii) If the head teacher is adamant in his refusal to accept that there is any justification for the managers' concern, the managers should draw the matter to the attention of the Authority by means of a resolution voted upon at a properly constituted managers' meeting.

Such a resolution could call upon the Authority to institute a full Inspection, or it could simply express in general terms the managers' concern about the school. As a result of such a resolution the Authority would almost certainly take some action. At the very least, it would ask the District Inspector to visit the school in order to determine if he can whether there is any justification for the managers' anxiety.

(iv) Following the intervention by the Authority in the form of the District Inspector's visit to the school, there are a number of possibilities that the managers may have to consider. First, the District Inspector and/or other representatives of the Authority may form the view that the managers' concern is justified, and may take steps which result in the head teacher remedying the position. Alternatively, the District Inspector and/or other representatives of the Authority may take the view that the managers are not justified in the concern that they have expressed, or, whilst accepting the justification for that concern, do insufficient to require the head teacher to remedy the position. In either of the latter two cases the managers have only two course of action properly open to them if they feel strongly about the matter. They are:

(a) to make a complaint against the head teacher and/or members of his staff for inefficiency, misconduct or indiscipline under the Authority's Disciplinary Procedures; or

(b) to invite the intervention of the Secretary of State, by requesting him to direct a local enquiry under Section 93 of the *1944 Act* and/or to refer the matter to the Secretary of State under Section 67 of the *1944 Act* for determination by him.

835. If managers are justified in their concern, and it is a matter of importance, the Authority would be gravely lacking in its duty if the managers were obliged to give expression to their responsiblities as managers by the institution of disciplinary proceedings or by referring the matter to the Secretary of State. Nevertheless, those are the steps which responsible managers should take in the interests of the school and the children in it if they feel strongly enough that some action should be taken.

Pressure on the Community

The second area in which you may want to exercise pressure is on the local community and its relations with the school. As you are probably a member of the local community yourself, you may know more than many of the teachers do about its needs and one function you can perform is to bring these to the notice of the school. You may also be in a better position to know the local reputation of the school. Often schools have a poorer reputation in their own immediate neighbourhood than they deserve, and governors can be very effective in attempting to counter this, by seeing there is an opportunity for local people to take part in school activities, by publicising the school's successes in the local paper, by encouraging the school to make good relationships with other local schools and community organisations, and by identifying themselves publicly with the school.

This pressure has to work both ways. You should also try to ensure that pressures from the community are properly felt by the school. Many, perhaps most, communities around schools are not homogenous, and here it is a question of making sure that the different communities in the school's neighbourhood are recognised and heard. There may be a number of different ethnic groups or different social groups, and some may have difficulty in communicating as vociferously as others. If you are not sure what the social, ethnic or economic composition of your area is, the local authority will probably have census data, broken down by ward.

This function of relating the school to the community may already be effectively performed by the PTA or parents' organisation if there is one. If it is there is obviously no purpose in duplication and the governors should identify themselves with the PTA's efforts. It is unlikely that any school will have good relations with the community as a whole unless it first establishes a good relationship with its parents, and it is an important part of the governors' functions to make sure that there are plenty of opportunities for parents and teachers to meet both formally and informally. You should ask for an account at every meeting of these occasions and from time to time initiate a discussion of the part parents play in the school and the success of various ways of trying to involve them. Parent governors themselves will obviously be particularly involved in this question.

Clearly the governors cannot serve any meaningful purpose in the parents' or the community's eyes unless the parents and community know who they are and what they do. It is up to the governors to make sure that their names and addresses are publicly displayed in some way – either on a school notice board or in the local library or distributed to all parents. It is also a good idea to make public some regular account of what the governors are doing. Parent governors and teacher governors will obviously be particularly concerned with reporting back to those who elected them, and may want to arrange for some regular opportunity to do this – a column in the school newsletter if there is one, and a 'slot' at PTA or staff association meetings. For dealing with many of a school's particular problems, whether it is the introduction and gaining acceptance of new teaching methods, or the need to mount a campaign for new buildings, the combined pressure of the staff association, the PTA and the governors can be formidably effective, as long as each group is aware of what the others are doing.

Pressure on the Local Authority

In order to bring pressure to bear effectively on the authority it is necessary to spend a little time understanding how the system of local government administration works. Any communication that you as a governor receive from the authority will probably be from the Director of Education (or Chief Education Officer). He is in effect the chief executive of the education authority and the letter will come from him in token of the fact that he has overall responsibility for the service, although if it is a routine matter it is almost certain that he has not in fact seen the letter. Under him are departments or branches responsible for particular sectors of the service: schools, further education, special education and so on, or for particular activities covering several of these sectors – the provision of school meals, and the Architect's Department for instance. If yours is a large authority there may also be officers responsible for the detailed adminstration of separate geographical areas within the authority's area, probably housed in offices within these areas, not at County Hall. It is the job of all these officers to keep the education service running efficiently, and any complaint or suggestion which you put to the authority in the form of a resolution at a governors' meeting will be submitted by your clerk to the appropriate department.

It is not the job of these officers to decide what the *policy* of the authority should be; this is the job of the Education Committee, which consists of the elected members of the local council. These people are, unlike Members of Parliament, not paid (except for an 'attendance allowance') and most of them have full-time jobs elsewhere. Even that time that they spend as elected councillors representing their constituents is spread over a number of committees, housing, social services etc, as well as education. They are therefore not in a position to carry out any detailed check on what the officers are doing, but the officers are none the less answerable to them.

You need therefore to contact your councillor (or member of the Education Committee), either when you want to influence a matter of policy (for instance whether the authority's schools should be co-educational or single-sex), or when you feel that the officers have not acted rightly or fairly in respect of some sort of representation you have made. It never does any harm to ask that a copy of a resolution on an important matter that your governing body has passed is sent to your local member, so that he can follow up what has happened to it. The local member should be familiar with the school in any case and it is a good idea to remind the head teacher to invite him to some school functions so that he and the school remain in touch. It is also open to you to ask that your resolutions be sent to the chairman of the relevant sub-committee of the authority. Sometimes it is worth seeing that all members of the relevant sub-committee are circulated. You can also ask any member to receive a deputation, or to attend a special meeting of the governors. Even if an officer attends instead, the fact that you are sufficiently persistent and serious in your demands to take it up in this way with your political representative may very well have an effect.

There is another type of officer within the local education service that should be explained; that is the inspector or adviser. There are several of these in all authorities, some attached to particular geographical areas, some in charge of sectors of the service and particular subject areas overall. They will probably spend a good deal of the time in schools, finding out how probationary teachers are faring, giving advice on curriculum development, checking on standards and morale generally. They will also probably spend time on committees and working parties do with the assessment and development of new curricular ideas. Another important part of their work is advising on appointments. In more progressive authorities they probably also see part of their job as explaining modern approaches to teaching to governors, parents and the public at large. It is well worth calling in their expertise to talk to the governors both at appointment meetings and on other occasions.*

If you have tried all approaches to effect some change in the educational

---

* Taylor recommended significant extension of their duties in this direction.

provision in your area and feel you are meeting a stone wall or cannot get the relevant people to meet you, it is always possible to use the local press.

Again, the Auld Report must be borne in mind. The managers there were censured for making their dispute with the head and staff public through the press – because Mr Auld felt that their actions were damaging to individual teachers and children. Obviously the situation is different where your problem is a battle over a non-personal problem, such as the need for new buldings or an objection to some plan of the Education Committee, in which governors and teachers are united. However, even here, it is almost always a mistake to write to the press or give them a 'story' before you have gone through the channels described above: this causes resentment and sours relations with officers and members. Nevertheless, as a last resort it can be effective.

Pressure on the Government

In one sense the strongest Government influence on education now rests not with the Secretary of State for Education, but with the Secretary of State for the Environment, since the latter most strongly influences how much each local authority may spend, and education is by far the largest element in local government spending.

But some elements in the education services are decided by the Secretary of State for Education and Science; the total amount of money available for teachers' salaries, for instance, and their qualifications. He has to approve, or otherwise, proposals to open, close or reorganise a school, and he also acts as adjudicator in cases of dispute between a governing body and its local education authority (Section 67 of the 1944 Education Act), and as an appeal tribunal against any local authority that acts or is proposing to act 'unreasonably' (Section 68). All that is needed to set this process in motion is a simple letter, invoking the Section, to the Secretary of State.

If there is a local matter in which any government department is acting in a way in which you feel to be damaging to the school, an important person to contact is your local Member of Parliament.

In all these cases where you are asking publicly elected figures for their advice and support, it is sensible as well as friendly to thank them if in fact they do their best to help you.

Chapter 17

Deputations

A deputation, as the word suggests, is a group of people deputed to be the spokesman of some larger group (in this case the governing body) in making some special case to the authority. To be an official deputation it has to be authorised by the body as a whole to make the approach: a self-appointed group cannot call themselves a deputation.

When the governing body decides to send a deputation, it has to settle two things: who is to go and what they are to ask for. The latter will often be self-evident, if it is a matter of getting an improvement on a building programme for instance, but sometimes a deputation is a wasted opportunity because its members have been charged only with making a complaint and not asking for anything specific. Make sure the governing body discusses what specifically it wants to come out of the deputation, and write it down. (It should be in the minutes of the meeting, but these may not reach you until after the deputation has taken place.) The important principle to follow when deciding who should go on a deputation is that all the interests on the governing body – parents, teachers, political nominees etc – should be represented. It is polite to let the person you are going to see know who is coming and what your business is.

The governors who have been chosen as the deputation should meet briefly after the governors' meeting to arrange the practical details: possible dates and times (the clerk should do the actual arranging), whether or not you need to take documentation with you or perhaps send it in advance, and when, if necessary, to have a briefing session. It is a useful practice to meet half an hour or so before the official time of the deputation in any case, whether or not a longer briefing session is necessary.

Before the deputation you should decide who is to 'lead', ie start off the discussion and introduce the other members; what points should be made, and by whom; and who is going to take notes of the meeting and write a minute afterwards. This does not mean that the occasion should be an entirely formal one; members of the deputation should not feel that they can say nothing except what was agreed beforehand, and you may actually get further if an atmosphere of informal conversation can be established; but it is essential to have an agreed list of points and make sure they are all covered.

A report of what was said at the meeting should be written as soon as possible and agreed by the other members of the deputation. It should in particular include any concessions made by the person you went to see. This should then be sent to the representatives of the authority present at the meeting, with a request that they should correct anything they do not agree is a correct record of what was said. If there are no corrections then the report should be sent to the rest of the governing body. The next meeting should then discuss it and decide on further action.

There may very well by somebody from the authority present at the deputation taking a note. It is wise to take your own as well: not because the official note will be incorrect or incomplete, but because you, knowing clearly what your local situation is and what you want, will be more sensitive to any possible concessions or new suggestions in what is said, and it is important to capture these and build on them. Of course, you can only do this if your report is an 'agreed' record, and that is why it is important to submit it to the authority before circulating it to fellow governors.

It is also important to send a letter of thanks after your meeting – even if you feel you got nothing out of it! You never know when in the future being remembered as a polite and friendly group of people may pay off.

Chapter 18

To Whom Are You Accountable?

Mention has been made throughout this book of the governors as bodies to whom the head and staff of a school are accountable. To whom are the governors accountable? The direct answer to this is: to the body that appoints them, ie in most cases the local education authority. Even if you are elected to your position by parents or teachers, your actual appointment, in the case of a county school, is by the authority, and the authority, under Section 21 of the 1984 Education Act, has the power to remove you. (In a voluntary school those governors appointed by the voluntary body concerned with the school are responsible to that body.)

The fact that you are responsible to the local education authority does not mean that you are not entirely free to criticise it. On the contrary, the Education Committee needs to be constantly informed of your grass-roots reactions to its policies. But it is right that the local, publicly elected, statutory body responsible for running the education service should have some sanction against any part of the local system that may abuse its powers. You are protected against the authority's abuse of its powers over you by your right of appeal to the Secretary of State.

Sections 67 and 68 of the Education Act, mentioned in the previous chapter, are a protection to all concerned against unreasonable behaviour. It is worth noting that Section 68 gives any aggrieved person a right of appeal to the Secretary of State, not only over the actions or proposed actions of the local education authority but also over such actions of any board of governors – so in this sense you are directly and legally responsible to the public at large. This again is as it should be.

If you have been appointed after election by one particular group within the school's community – say, the parents – then it is only natural that you should feel in some sense accountable to them. You will want to report back to them on what is happening, and it is your special function to represent their interests. However, you are not a delegate, and do not have to seek a mandate on all issues that arise. On some matters a canvass of opinion might help you to make up your own mind, but once you are on the governing body, you are a governor in your own right, not only a spokesman.

Chapter 19

Special Schools

Special schools, both day and boarding, offer education for children with difficulties who cannot be educated satisfactorily in an ordinary school. Places in special schools are offered to those pupils who have been formally 'assessed' as in need of a particular form of special education. Maintained special schools are run by local education authorities; non-maintained special schools are run by voluntary bodies whose expenditure is met primarily by fees charged to the authorities whose pupils they take (and there may be some grant from the DES for buildings and equipment).

Since 1981 it has been official policy to try to accomodate children with special educational needs in ordinary schools and to concentrate, in both ordinary and special schools, on the education of the whole child. Words like 'handicap' are officially avoided, and there are no longer official categories of handicap. Special schools accomodate children who are blind or partially sighted, deaf or partially hearing, physically disabled or with emotional and behavioural difficulties and moderate or severe learning difficulties. The latter are those who used to be called 'mentally handicapped': where they are in hospitals, the local education authorities have since 1971 been responsible for their education.

If you are the governor of a special school you have two separate but connected concerns. The first will be to act as a governor of the school, just as you would if it were any ordinary maintained school. The second is to understand the particular needs of the children concerned. The children in the school themselves have two needs: first, to be helped with their difficulty; second, the general needs they have in common with other children. One of your concerns therefore is to help to promote a balance within the school between that part of the child's education which has to do with special techniques and organisation, and that which offers these children the opportunites and environment to be found in the best schools for normal children.

This dual concern may be expressed in a number of ways. For example, in appointing staff you will need to be particularly sensitive to an applicant's attitudes towards the difficulty. You need to consider whether he is so concerned with the difficulty as to lose sight of the children as people – or whether, caring for people, he is too inexperienced to manage the difficulty or understand its implications.

Another example concerns the curriculum. It is important that the general capacities of children with physical difficulties are not under-estimated. One question is whether the school is able to offer them the same opportunites as normal schools for taking external examinations. Governors may have a role here in helping to raise the academic expectations in the school.

It is important that you become as informed as possible about the particular difficulty with which your school is concerned. This preperation should focus on its educational and medical implications. Training for governors of special schools is particularly urgent.

In the absence of such training there are a number of sources of information. The first is the head and staff of the school. Your sensitive requests for help from them will not only lead to your being better informed, but will help them to formulate their problems and discuss the solutions which they and others propose. You can ask the head and staff to direct you to good sources of literature and other information.

It would also be a help to join the local branch of the voluntary organisation which represents parents dealing with the particular difficulty. This will not only give you information, it will introduce you to the parents' point of view about schools in general and perhaps about your own school in particular. If there is no such organisation locally there are numerous national societies whose names you can get through the Disabled Living Foundation, 380 Harrow Road, London W9 2HU, 01-289 6111.

You may also get considerable help from your local health visitor. She may be particularly informative about the medical aspects and implications. Now that the school health service is administered by area health authorities, you may find that you have a particular part to play in ensuring that education is not hampered by inadequate medical information and help. Teachers of children with difficulties frequently complain that they do not receive proper medical information: governors can support them by making appropriate representatations to the area health authority. The more background information you have on this, the more effective you will be.

The growth of your knowledge will have two other important effects. It will encourage the staff who may feel that their work is undervalued or misunderstood and it will help to diminish some of the unhealthy mysticism which can attach to special education. Staff in special schools can often feel isolated. It can be a great help to them to feel that the governors are sufficiently knowledgeable to make a genuine discussion of their problems and proposals useful and productive.

Another task which is common to schools in general but assumes particular importance in special schools is the fostering of links between the school and the community it serves. The problems here are obvious. The low incidence of many difficulties means that many children come to special schools by bus from quite far afield. In this sense the school cannot be a neighbourhood school, and it may indeed seem foreign or even threatening to the people in the area. You may have read of newspaper reports where a local population gets up a campaign against the siting of a school or for the removal of an existing one. In these circumstances your job of representing the school to its locality is a formidable one.

There are authorities which group their special schools together so that several quite different schools accomodating widely differing needs share the same governing body. Under these circumstances it is very hard for governors to give a high standard of individual care to a particular special school. It is open to you to press the authority to establish separate boards of governors for individual schools.

Clearly, the work of special schools is affected by a large number of specialisms from different disciplines, some of whom may be attached to the school itself. These include child care staff, therapists, nurses, doctors, psychologists, social workers and so on. It is an important question how far these staff should be represented on the governing bodies of schools and how far they should attend as specialist advisers. It is important to you as a governor to be sure that you are aware of the views of such specialists, not only on the specialisms, but on the general working of the school itself.

It is obviously not possible in this handbook to discuss individual handicaps and the complicated educational issues they raise. But there are a number of points which may seem routine but which can make a great difference to the experience of pupils. For example, the arrangements for transport are a matter for the local authority, but a governing body should try to see that they are adequate and make representations if they are not. Children may spend as much as two hours a day on the school bus. It is important to see that buses and taxis do not habitually arrive late or leave early.

The question of suspension is particularly difficult in special schools, and the governors should try to be sure that the alternative arrangements made for a suspended or expelled pupil are satisfactory.

Such matters as diet are important too, where children are immobile and have weight problems.

More generally important is the question of links between home and school and how these can be encouraged when parents live far away. It may be possible to encourage the relevant voluntary or parents' organisation to use the school building out of school hours. Your concern for the curriculum may lead you to see how far the teachers of children with severe communication problems use any form of home-school notebook.

These suggestions are general ones, offering ways in which you may begin to tackle the task of being not only a good governor of a school but a sensitive and humane governor of a special school for children with special educational needs.

Chapter 20

Arguments About the Role and Functions of Governors

For the last ten years or more there has been considerable argument and discussion about the composition and functions of governing bodies. By far the most substantial account of the issues, together with recommendations for action, appeared in *A New Partnership for Our Schools*, the Report of a Committee of Inquiry appointed by the Secretaries of State for Education and Science and for Wales (the Taylor Report). Since its publication in 1977, there has been legislation (the Education Act, 1980) and further proposals from the Government culminating in the White Paper *Better Schools* (Cmnd 9469) published in March 1985.

The main issue in the composition of governing bodies is whether any of the varying interests surrounding the school (parents, teachers, LEA) should command a majority. The Taylor Report proposed that these interests should have equal shares and together co-opt a fourth from the local community. The 1985 White Paper provides for a rather smaller representation of teachers.

On functions, the discussion has centred round the nature of the governors' responsibility and the need to distinguish clearly between their functions and those of the head on one side and the LEA on the other. The Government's latest proposals are that this should be embodied, in considerable detail, in legislation.

These proposals raise another general issue: how far should legislation provide a broad framework, leaving detailed arrangements to the instruments and articles of individual schools, and how far should it specify detail itself? The former allows for greater local flexibility and initiative. The latter would attempt to improve clarity and understanding through universal prescription. This would increase the Secretary of State's detailed control of school government.

For much of the time governors may not be interested in or even aware of these running controversies, but it often happens that events relating to a particular school raise questions about the principles on which governors are acting. It is thus important for governors to be aware of issues of school government and of what have been and may be the principles on which they are required to operate. The following chapters thus summarise the Taylor Report, the response to it made by the National Association of Governors and Managers and the proposals in the White Paper *Better Schools*.

Chapter 21

Summary of the Taylor Report

Principles

The Taylor Report sets out six principles which governed its recommendations:

1. Within the framework of national and local policies the special character of the individual school is precious to most people and should be protected.
2. That character is a product of local considerations and of the skill, support and concern of local people.
3. One body should have delegated responsibility for running the school, and in that body no one interest should be dominant: it should be a secure partnership of local education authority, staff, parents, pupils where appropriate, and the community.
4. The governing body should be responsible for the life and work of the school as a whole: neither the school's activity nor accountability for its success could be divided.
5. Promoting and protecting good relationships within the school and between the school and its parents and community was as important a function of the governing body as making decisions.
6. The details of any new arrangements for governing bodies could be left to local discretion but their essential features should be universal.

General

All the powers relating to school government should be formally invested in the local education authority, but there should be as much delegation of these powers by the authority to the governing body as was compatible with the authority's responsibility for providing and maintaining the schools in its area. In turn, the governing body should give to head teachers as much discretion as is compatible with the governors' responsibility for the success of the school. Every school should have its own separate governing body, and the terms governing body and governors should apply to both primary and secondary schools.

Membership

Membership of governing bodies should consist of equal numbers of local authority representatives, school staff, parents (with, where appropriate, pupils) and representatives of the local community. There should not be less than two members in any one category and there should not normally be more than 24 members in all. The representation of minor authorities on the managing bodies of primary schools should end.

Elected members of local authorities might be appointed in either the 'local education authority' or 'community' category. The head should always be a member of the governing body and included *ex officio* among the staff representatives. Priority for the staff places should be given to teachers: representatives of supporting staff should be included where size permits. Teaching and other staff representatives should be elected by the staff concerned. Those to be appointed as parent governors should be elected by the parents of the children attending the school: the rules and procedures for their election should be made by the local education authority. These elections should be school-based, should seek to ensure maximum participation and should satisfy the following criteria: comunications should be in plain words; every parent should be eligible to nominate candidates, to stand for election and to cast one vote; nomination and voting papers, and the results of the election, should be sent to every parent.

The Secretaries of State should take definitive advice on the law to enable pupils to serve as members at 16; and senior secondary pupils to participate in school government to the fullest extent allowed by law until they were clearly eligible for membership.

The representatives of the community should be co-opted by the governors representing the three other interest groups. A local education authority might draw up lists of people willing to serve and in doing so should invite local employers or business organisations and trade unions to submit nominations.

Nobody should serve as the governor of more than one school in any given age group.

Communication and Cooperation

A number of recommendations for improving communication between governors and authority, staff, parents, pupils and the community include requesting the head teacher to submit proposals for consultation with staff; authorising the establishment of a school council by the pupils; giving parents the opportunity to set up an organisation for themselves and making the governors' views available in consultations with the local authority.

Curriculum

The governors should have the responsibility for setting the aims of the school, for considering the means by which they are produced, for reviewing the school's progress towards them and for deciding on action to help that progress. They should invite the head in consultation with staff to prepare papers on the means by which they propose to pursue the aims adopted.

Within the framework of local authority policy, the governing body should formulate guidelines for standards of behaviour and rules and sanctions necessary to maintain them. Individual governors should be able to see classes at work, under arrangements agreed with the staff.

One of the authority's general advisers should be regularly available for each school and able to report to the governing body on request. Authorities should review their advisory and inspection services in the light of this.

The governing body should be kept unobtrusively informed of the life and activities of the school and should produce a first general appraisal of the school's progress within four years of its formation and subsequent appraisals at agreed intervals. A short report on these appraisals should be sent to the local authority.

Finance

The governors should have the responsibility for initiating the estimates in a school, as provided in the model articles of 1945. Financial arrangements should facilitate initiative and independent action at the school level. Authorities should consult governing bodies before deciding on building work at their schools and during the subsequent planning and building stages.

Appointments

Heads should be appointed by a small selection committee consisting equally of governors and representatives of the authority. The committee should elect its own chairman, who should have a casting vote.

The selection of deputy heads and other teachers should rest with the governing body with regard both to professional advice and the responsibility of the authority to employ teachers whose schools are closed or reorganised. Governing bodies should have access to the authority's Staff Code relating to teachers.

The Secretaries of State should discuss with local authority associations and teachers' associations the problem of teachers who find it hard to meet their professional obligations.

Suspensions

The report makes detailed recommendations about suspension. It suggests that expulsion should be taken to mean permanent debarment from school; exclusion should mean temporary debarment on medical grounds and suspension should be temporary debarment for other reasons.

Legislation should ensure that only the local authority can decide to expel a pupil, informing the governing body of its decision, and that no pupil is suspended (ie debarred on other than medical grounds) except in compliance with the local authority's suspension procedures. These procedures should provide consultation with parents if suspension is contemplated; should make clear who can decide on suspension; should provide that suspension should be for no longer than three days with provision to avoid danger to the pupil or others;

should provide that a decision to suspend should be quickly and reliably communicated to parents and entered in a register in the school; should give the governing body power to extend the suspension for a limited period specified by the authority during which interested parties can have discussions: if these discussions fail the case should be referred to the local authority; and should provide for an appeal by parents.

Premises

Governors should continue to be responsible for inspecting the premises and for informing the authority of their conditions and state of repair. They should also have the power to carry out urgent minor repairs up to a limit set by the authority.

Other Functions

The present arrangements for admissions should continue, and the authority should make public the principles and criteria on which its admissions policy is based.

The local authority, after consulting governing bodies, should formulate an overall policy on school lettings and the governing body should give the head teacher guidelines for considering applications to use the school premises. In any dispute between the governing body and an outside organisation the final decision should rest with the authority.

Governing bodies should continue to have the power to grant occasional school holidays.

Training

All education authorities should make initial and in-service training courses available to governors, and as soon as practicable all governors should have a short period of initial training and attend in-service training courses regularly. The local authority should designate a person responsible for coordinating the training of governors.

Procedural Arrangements

Regular meetings of the governing body should be held at least twice a term. Additional meetings of the governing body should require the agreement of at least one-third of the members. Times of meetings should be decided by the governors themselves.

Proceedings of the meetings should not be confidential unless the governing body specifically so decides in regard to a particular item of its business. Confidential items in the minutes should be recorded separately.

Agenda, reports and minutes of governing bodies should be sent to the authority and to all members of the body itself. Information about membership should be made widely available to parents and others. Governors should be able to elect any one of their members as chairman except paid members of the staff.

The local authority should decide on the system of clerking governing bodies.

Allowances for loss of earnings, for travelling and incidental expenses should be payable to all governors but attendance allowances should not be payable.

Voluntary Schools

Recommendations which do not affect the principle of the 'dual system' should be applied by those concerned equally in voluntary as in county schools, and the Secretaries of State should consult the providing bodies and others with a view to adopting arrangements along the lines proposed.

Implementation

Legislation should give all authorities the duty to make arrangements for the government of county schools in line with the Taylor recommendations. The local authorities should report within five years on the working of these arrangements. The Secretaries of State should at the same time monitor progress through an independent agency.

Notes of Extension and Dissent

Seven members of the Committee added a note of extension in which they recommended that each individual parent should have the right in law to information about the performance of his legal duty to see that his child is educated. This would include information about the school generally, regular consultation and reports on the child, the opportunity to see teachers, guidance on supporting the school and access to information about his own child, including reports kept in a permanent form in the school.

One member entered a note of dissent on three issues. He thought that the recommendations on finance were unrealistic and unworkable and the recommendations on the appointment of deputy heads and other teachers should be more at the discretion of the local authority. He was also against clarifying or changing the law to permit pupil governors from the age of 16.

Minority Report

One member of the Committee declined to sign the report and wrote a letter and minority report of his own. Broadly he thought the recommendations were impractical and would give too much information to teachers. He wished to see no more authority taken away from the local education authority and the head teacher. He made his own proposals for the composition and functions of governing bodies.

This summary of the main recommendations of the Taylor Committee is included here for the convenience of users of the handboook. Serous governors will read the report itself, *A New Partnership for our Schools*, Department of Education and Science, (HMSO) Sept 1977, £3.25.

Chapter 22

Response of the NAGM to the Taylor Report

Dear Secretary of State,

We are very grateful for the chance to comment upon the proposals of the Taylor Committee which is offered by your letter of October 6, 1977. We welcome your statement on the importance of school governing bodies, their role as links between school and community and the need for parent and teacher involvement in them. We also welcome your acceptance of the Committee's recommendations on the composition and mode of appointment of governing and managing bodies, and your readiness to legislate to this end.

We hope it will be helpful if, in this report, we state our Association's views on legislation in general, on the specific four points you raise and upon the separate issues of suspension and voluntary schools.

On legislation in general, our Association has always inclined to the view that most of the changes that are needed in government can be brought about within existing legislation. We believe that the distribution of powers and duties, among parents, local authorities and the Secretaries of State, are broadly right, and that it is important not to upset the balance. We have, therefore, proposed the minimum changes that we believe to be necessary. We believe the Taylor proposals can be similarly accomodated. Above all, we are anxious that legislation should not be so detailed as to inhibit further development and innovation. Our detailed proposals are attached in Annexe 1.

On you four specific questions, our Association would propose:

(i) That the Taylor proposals be accepted, particularly as regards the 'four equal shares' formula. We support the idea that the fourth share should be co-opted by the other three, but we are doubtful about the idea of a local authority list from which such co-option should be made. If this list is merely an indication that certain people from certain backgrounds are ready to serve, well and good. But it should not mean that governing bodies cannot co-opt other people if they wish. In other words, responsibility for co-option should rest with the governors, and the list should not be exclusory.

(ii) That the logic of our own proposals for the composition of governing bodies leads to the effective end of the power of minor authorities to appoint managers. We had earlier proposed that the minor authorities should appoint in the same way as the education authorities – after elections by parents and teachers. But we recognised that this was a cumbersome device which derived from the existence of the minor authority's powers. We recognise that under the Taylor proposals this power of the minor authority would be anomalous. We believe that the local interest which is meant to be secured by it would be better represented by the school-based Taylor proposals. But we think it might be a useful convention for the education authority to appoint one of its own governors after consultation with the minor authority. There is, after all, no longer any question of the balance of control as between local authorities, but this kind of representation of the minor authority might have advantages.

(iii) That it should be accepted that pupils under 18 might be governors. Our Association has taken its own legal advice and has noted the experience of a number of authorities which have governors under 18. An article by one of our committee members is attached as Appendix 2 [not included here]. This sets out what we believe to be the present state of affairs. In some ways we believe that it would be enough to leave the matter to be tested in the courts. If you think legislation is essential then it should provide that pupils under 18 should not be precluded from being governors or carrying out the functions of governors by virtue of their age.

(iv) That the proposed limitation might prove awkward in practice. The principle behind it we entirely support; that individuals should not be able to accumulate governorships, but this is less likely under the Taylor proposals anyway. It may be, however, that in an area it might be possible for each secondary school to have a councillor for a governor, provided some councillors had two schools. If this were thought desirable it would be a pity to have a law against it. We use this only as an example, but it illustrates our general concern lest legislation should be so detailed as to preclude desirable local variants and experiments.

On the suspension of pupils, our Association's discussion paper is attached as Appendix 3 [not included here]. From this it will be seen that we broadly support the Taylor proposals on procedures. The present position is in many ways unsatisfactory and we would welcome quick improvement. Where we seem to differ from Taylor is in our view of the role of the local education authority. In our procedures the governors would recommend exclusion and the authority would make alternative provision. Under Taylor there is a proposal that there should be an appeal by the parents to the authority. This seems to bring confusion into the authority's role. There is such a wide variety of alternative provision made these days that authorities have fewer problems in placing difficult pupils. An appeal, if one is to be made, should probably be to the Secretary of State: this would certainly accord with the provisions of Section 68 of the Education Act, 1944.

Finally, on voluntary schools, our Association's general views are attached in our Discussion Paper as Appendix 4 [not included here]. We accept the principle that parents, pupils and teachers should be accomodated on voluntary school governing bodies as on maintained school ones. We do not think that the difficulties are as great as your Department seems to be advising. The clue to a solution probably lies in distinguishing between trustees and governors, and in suggesting to the trustees that, so far as the appointment of governors is concerned they act in the same way as the local authority, taking one quarter of the places and making the rest available to parents (pupils), teachers and co-options as Taylor recommends. There are already voluntary schools with few trustees on the governing body. In seeking to reflect the various interests concerned with the school (which is what the Taylor proposals seek to do) the trustees and the local authority might share the 'authority' quarter, or the governing body might be divided into five, with the trustees' and the authority's share of the two-fifths being in the present proportions allotted to aided and controlled schools respectively. But in this the numbers are of less importance than the principle that the increased representation of parents, pupils and teachers is possible.

We hope these replies have been helpful and we should be pleased to expand or explain them at a meeting with you or your officers if this seemed apt.

November 1977   *David Drown*
                                                       CHAIRMAN

Annexe 1

PROPOSALS FOR LEGISLATION

At present the 1944 Act lays down the powers, duties and manner of appointing of governors only in the broadest outline. The details are filled in by the instruments of management or government and the rules of management or articles of government of particular schools. After 1944 the Ministry of Education issued model instruments and rules or articles, and this model has been very widely followed since. The practice of leaving the detail out of legislation has the advantage that diversity, flexibility and innovation become possible. The Association would not wish any legislation introduced which would make future improvement more difficult than it has been in the past. However, legislation could usefully lay down minimum requirements within which local education authorities could make detailed local arrangements for the composition, functions and structure of school government machinery: such legislation should make the representation of parents and teachers on all governing and managing bodies mandatory. Some detailed changes in the composition of boards of government and management would also require new legislation. We accordingly propose that:

(i)   Sections 18 and 19 of the Act be amended so as to provide that in the case of both primary and secondary schools the governing body should consist of at least eight members.

(ii) Sections 18 and 19 of the Act be amended so that where reference is made to the local education authorities' power of appointment it should in every case be made clear that that power can be exercised by its delegation to some other group of persons who shall be entitled to elect representatives to the governing body. Thus, for example, S19(1) might have added at the end of it the words: 'or elected by such persons as the local education authority may nominate'. It is appreciated that the present wording of the Act does not prevent

85

the local education authority's exercising its power of appointment in this way (and has not done so), but an express statutory reference to this possibility would make the practice more secure.

(iii)   A fresh provision should be included in the Act requiring the list of governors or managers and their addresses to be kept in the school and to be available on request during school hours.

(iv)   Section 20 of the 1944 Act should be repealed.

(v)   A new Adminsitrative Memorandum should be issued enclosing new model instruments, articles of government and rules of management. These should provide for election of teachers, parents and community representatives to be appointed to governing bodies, as well as direct appointees of the local authorities. The proportions of the different elements on the governing body should be specified, and outline machinery should be included laying down how the elections of representatives of the parents and staff should take place.

Chapter 23

The Government's Proposals 1985

In the years following the publication of the Taylor Report there was much discussion about the composition and functions of governing bodies. Composition was the subject of legislation in the Education Act, 1980, the provisions of which represent the present legal position and are described on pages 12–14 above. Broadly, they accommodate representation of parents and teachers on governing bodies, though not to the extent which the Taylor Committee recommended.

Not long after the Act was passed, and before it had been fully implemented, the Government thought again, and a Green Paper, *Parental Influence at School* (Cmnd 9242), published in May 1984, proposed that parent representatives should be able to form the majority on governing bodies. This suggestion was almost universally opposed. (At about the same time the Government also proposed that the majority of governing bodies in inner London should be held by representatives of inner London boroughs, and this suggestion was also widely opposed.)

In March 1985 the Government published a White Paper, *Better Schools* (Cmnd 9469), in which it made new proposals both for the composition of governing bodies and also for clarifying their functions. A summary of these proposals follows.

The Government's proposals cover county and voluntary controlled schools only and are explicitly stated to be introduced in the interest of raising standards in school education.

Composition

The proposed composition of governing bodies for county, voluntary controlled and maintained special schools is given in the table overleaf.

THE PROPOSED COMPOSITION OF GOVERNING BODIES FOR COUNTY, VOLUNTARY CONTROLLED AND MAINTAINED SPECIAL SCHOOLS

Size of school	Elected by and from parents [b]	Appointed by LEA	Head-teacher [c]	Elected by and from teachers	Co-opted [d] or, for controlled schools: Foundation / Co-opted [d]		Total
fewer than 100 pupils	2	2	1	1	3 — 2	1	9
100–299 pupils	3	3	1	1	4 — 3	1	12
300 pupils or more [a]	4	4	1	2	5 — 4	1	16
600 pupils or more [a]	5	5	1	2	6 — 4	2	19

Notes
(a) the LEA would be free to choose either composition for schools with 600 or more pupils.
(b) where insufficient parents stood for election (or, in any case, for schools with at least 50 per cent boarders) the LEA would appoint parent proxies to fill vacancies. LEA members and employees and co-opted members of the Education Committee would be inelegible for such proxy appointments.
(c) the headteacher would be able to choose not to be a governor.
(d) the number of co-optees would be reduced by one to allow for the addition shown in the following mutually exclusive circumstances:
    (i) one representative of the minor authority (or minor authorities, acting jointly) in the case of a county or controlled primary school serving an area in which there is one or more minor authorities;
    (ii) one representative of the District Health Authority in the case of a hospital special school;
    (iii) one representative of a relevant voluntary organisation in the case of any other maintained special school.

The principles on which this composition are based are: no single interest (parents, teachers nor LEA) would predominate; the existing representation of teachers, foundations and minor authorities is preserved; there would be co-opted governors; the bodies would be small enough for efficient action; and the application of the provisions to individual schools should be by instruments of government. The Government also proposed that the LEA should fill parent governor vacancies, if too few parents came forward; that governors' term of office should be four years; that parent governors would complete their term of office after their children have left the school; the grouping of two primary schools would require the Secretary of State's approval; and there would be 'shadow' governing bodies for new schools.

Functions – Principles and General Powers

The White Paper confirmed the principles on which its proposals were based; the LEA must have sufficient powers to carry out its duties for providing schools and for determining overall policy; the governing body should determine, in consultation with the head, the main policies and lines of development of the school; the professional responsibilties of the head teacher and staff must be clear and respected; and there should be no distinction between primary and secondary schools. On general powers, the White Paper said that the governors would have a duty to report to the LEA, and the head a duty to report both to the governing body and to the LEA. In urgent matters the chairman of governors would be empowered to act for the whole body.

Conduct and Curriculum

Responsibility for the general direction of the conduct of the school would be given to the governing body. On curriculum, the LEA would be responsible for curricular policy; the governing body would set out, with the advice of the head and after consultation with the LEA, the school's curricular aims and objectives; the head would be responsible for 'the organisation and delivery' of the curriculum, including syllabuses, teaching methods and materials, within available resources and in the light of the aims and objectives.

On discipline the Government proposed that the head could formulate rules and sanctions in the light of guidance from the governors; the governors and the head must consult the LEA on any disciplinary issue involving additional public expenditure or affecting the LEA's responsibilities as employer. If a head excluded a pupil for more than three days or so as to prevent the pupil taking a public examination he must inform the governing body and the LEA. Both the governors and the LEA could direct the head to end the exclusion, and such direction for the LEA would be binding on the governors and the head. If the LEA believed that order in a school had broken down or was about to do so it might take the necessary steps to ensure order.

Staffing Matters

Under the White Paper proposals, a head teacher would be selected by a panel on which the governing body had the same number of members as the LEA (three each) or a majority. The panel would recommend one candidate to the LEA for appointment, though the LEA, as the employer, could decline to make the appointment. The procedure for appointment, including determining the requirements of the post, the advertisement to be placed and the selection arrangements to be followed, would be the subject of legislation.

For an assistant teacher, the LEA would determine whether a vacant post existed and whether it should be filled by public advertisement, from a recruitment or redeployment pool or by the redeployment of a teacher from another school. If the post were to be advertised the governing body would select a candidate for appointment by the LEA, but could delegate this responsibility to the head teacher. If the post were not advertised the governing body might draw up a specification for the post which the LEA would have to take into account. If the governors did not accept any of the offered candidates that LEA must consider their representations and if it overruled them it must report this fact to the next meeting of the education committee. A similar procedure would be followed for both deputy head teachers and for non-teaching staff.

Staff dismissals would be a matter for the local authority but the LEA would be required first to consult the governors and head. It must also consider any recommendation from a governing body that a member of staff should be dismissed. The LEA, the governing body and the head would also have the power to suspend a member of staff, and the LEA would decide on the action to be taken.

It would be for the LEA to decide such matters as premature retirement, redundancy, redeployment and the outcome of probation but the LEA would be required to consult the governors and the head before doing so.

Finance

The LEA, says the White Paper, must be ultimately responsible for the effective management of money but there should be a measure of delegation of financial responsibility to schools. The LEA would be required to give the governing body an itemised statement of recurrent expenditure on the school. It would also be required to allocate a sum to the governing body to spend at its discretion on books, equipment and stationery, subject to the LEA's financial rules. The LEA would be free to allocate to the governors responsibility for other items. The Government says that it would be sensible for the governing body to delegate the expenditure of this money to the head teacher, who would then account to the governors for the exercise of discretion.

Other Functions

The White Paper does not propose any significant change in responsibility for premises and admissions. It suggests that the clerk to the governing body should be appointed by the LEA (though he would not be an officer) after consultation with the governing body.

Annual Report and Parents' Meeting

The White Paper proposes that a governing body should issue an annual report of its activities, and the Government would specify in legislation both that the report should be brief and its minimum contents. Governors would be asked to consider the desirability of publishing the report in English or Welsh, 'as appropriate', and governors might consider translations into other languages.

Governors would be required to call an annual meeting of parents to discuss their report and other matters relating to the life of the school. The meeting would be able to pass resolutions which the head, the governors or the LEA must consider and report back on. The quorum for the meeting would be 10 per cent of eligible parents.

Support and Training for Governors

The Government would require LEAs to give every governor a copy of the school's instrument and articles of government together with other explanatory and background material and would be required to secure training for governors free of charge.

Instruments and Articles

The changes proposed in the White Paper would mean that for the first time considerable detail on composition and functions of governing bodies would be incorporated in the law. It is proposed, therefore, to simplify the arrangements for making instruments and articles of government. Briefly, the LEAs would be responsible for making and amending these for all maintained schools in their areas, after consultation with the governing body of the school concerned, or the shadow governing body of a new school. In any dispute between the LEA and the governors the Secretary of State's decision would be binding.

Voluntary Aided and Special Agreement Schools

No changes are proposed in the composition of governing bodies of voluntary aided and special agreement schools, though shadow arrangements for new voluntary aided schools would be established. The new powers and duties of governing bodies in respect of discipline, finance, the annual report and parents' meeting, information, and training of governors would be applied to governing bodies of aided and special agreement schools, modified as appropriate. Before publishing admission agreements the governors of these schools would be required to consult the LEA annually. Control of the 'secular curriculum' in aided and special agreement primary schools would be vested in the governors, as it is now in secondary schools.

Future legislation would also accomodate the possibility of controlled schools becoming aided schools. The detailed procedure would be broadly analogous to that relating to changes in the character of schools under Section 13 of the 1980 Act.

Allowances for Governors

The White Paper proposed that, on the general principle that service as a governor should be regarded as voluntary service, legislation will empower, but not oblige, LEAs to pay travelling and subsistence allowances to governors. It would permit differentiation between different kinds of institution (like schools and colleges) but not between governors of a single institution. It would permit LEAs to set upper and lower mileage limits so as to disallow excessive and trivial claims.

Resources and Guidance

The White Paper estimated that additional costs arising from the proposed changes would be about £10m in a full year. The Government proposed to issue guidance on the detailed application of new arrangements and was considering offering grants for pilot projects to develop models of good practice in the training of governors.

Appendix A
Extracts from the Education (School Premises) Regulations 1981

PART III

School accommodation – provisions of general application

7. **Buildings** The buildings provided for a school shall be adequate to permit not only the provision of accomodation satisfying the requirements of this Part (and, in the case of a school with boarding pupils, of Part IV) but also of the provision of appropriate ancillary facilities, in particular –

   (a) for the convenient passage of persons and movement of goods within the buildings;
   (b) for the storage, in or near the teaching accommodation, of apparatus, equipment and materials used in teaching;
   (c) for the storage, elsewhere than in the teaching accommodation, of such things not presently used in teaching or used for maintenance or other purposes and of furniture;
   (d) for the separate storage of any fuel required for the purposes of the school;
   (e) for storing and drying pupils' outdoor clothing and for storing their other belongings; and
   (f) for the preparation of food and drinks and the washing of crockery and other utensils.

8. **Teaching accommodation** (1) The school building shall include teaching accommodation of a net area not less than the minimum for the school determined in accordance with Schedule 4.

(2) Without prejudice to paragraph (1), the net area of the teaching

accommodation at a special school shall be such as takes account of the special educational needs of the pupils thereat.

(3) For the purposes hereof 'teaching accommodation' means accommodation provided for teaching purposes except that in relation to a nursery school or class it includes playroom accommodation, and in relation to teaching accommodation, 'net area' means the floor area less so much thereof as is used for the purposes mentioned in Regulation 7 (a) or (b).

9. Accommodation for private study and social purposes for pupils who have attained the age of 16 years (1) This Regulation shall apply in the case of a school with pupils who have attained the age of 16 years.

(2) In the case of such a school the buildings shall include, within the teaching accommodation, accommodation to be used by such pupils for private study and social purposes, the minimum floor area of which shall be $0.2m^3$ for each such pupil.

10. Washrooms etc. – pupils (1) In this and the next following Regulation – 'the basic number' shall not be less than four but, subject as aforesaid, means, in relation to a school other than a special school, the aggregate of –
- (a) a tenth of the number of pupils thereat who have not attained the age of 5 years, and
- (b) a twentieth of the number of pupils thereat who have attained that age, and, in relation to a special school, a tenth of the number of pupils thereat, in each case rounded up to the nearest whole even number;

'sanitary fitting' means a water closet or, in the case of a school attended by boys, a water closet or urinal;

'washroom' means a room containing sanitary fittings and washbasins.

(2) In every school there shall be washrooms, for pupils, which taken together contain not less than the basic number of sanitary fittings and –
- (a) in the case of a school at which the majority of the pupils have attained the age of 11 years, each washroom shall contain at least two washbasins for each three sanitary fittings therein;
- (b) in the case of any other school, the number of washbasins shall not be less then the basic number.

(3) In washrooms provided for boys not more than two thirds of the sanitary fittings provided in pursuance of paragraph (2) shall be urinals.

(4) In the case of a school with pupils who have not attained the age of 5 years, one deep sink shall be provided for every 40 such pupils, the number of such pupils being rounded up to the nearest multiple of 40.

(5) Subject to paragraph (7), changing accommodation shall be provided for pupils who have attained the age of 8 years and are in receipt of physical education and the said accommodation shall be –
  (a) readily accessible from the school grounds, and
  (b) if accommodation for physical education is provided within the school buildings, also readily accessible from that accommodation.

(6) The changing accommodation provided in pursuance of paragraph (5) for pupils who have attained the age of 11 years shall include showers.

(7) In relation to a primary school (including a school deemed to be a primary school in pursuance of section 1 (2) of the Education Act 1964) paragraph (5) shall not apply if the school consists wholly or mainly of existing buildings.

11. Washroom etc. – staff (1) In this Regulation 'staff', in relation to a school, includes both teachers and other persons employed thereat and separate provision shall be made, in pursuance thereof, for male and female staff, such provision being separate from the provision made for pupils in pursuance of Regulation 10.

(2) In every school there shall be classrooms and washrooms for the staff.

(3) In the case of a school with pupils who have attained the age of 8 years, changing accommodation and showers shall be provided for members of the staff engaged in physical education.

12. Medical accommodation (1) In every school there shall be accommodation for the medical or dental examination and treatment of pupils by doctors, dentists or nurses and for the care of pupils during school hours.

(2) The accommodation provided in pursuance of this Regulation shall contain a washbasin and be reasonably near a water closet.

(3) Account may be taken for the purposes of this Regulation of accommodation (not being teaching accommodation) provided otherwise than for the purposes mentioned in paragraph (1) which is both appropriate and readily available for those purposes, in particular, in the case of a boarding school, of sick room accommodation provided in Regulation 19.

TABLE

Teaching accommodation at schools other than nursery schools and special schools

Relevant total number of pupils (within the meaning of paragraph 3 (2)(a) – entries to be construed inclusive of both numbers specified)	Minimum area in square metres for each pupil				
	Pupils who have not attained the age of 9 years	Pupils who have attained the age of 9 but not that of 11 years	Pupils who have attained the age of 11 but not that of 13 years	Pupils who have attained the age of 13 but not that of 15 years	Pupils who have attained the age of 15 years (including pupils who have attained any higher age)
80 or less	1.80	1.80	3.72	4.65	5.20
81 to 120	2.77	3.13	3.72	4.65	5.20
121 to 150	2.61	2.89	3.72	4.65	5.20
151 to 180	2.54	2.77	3.72	4.65	5.20
181 to 300	2.38	2.58	3.62	4.55	5.11
301 to 450	2.24	2.43	3.62	4.55	5.11
451 to 520	2.21	2.38	3.62	4.55	5.11
521 to 700	2.19	2.34	3.53	4.46	5.02
701 to 800		2.31	3.48	4.41	4.97
801 to 900			3.39	4.32	4.88
901 to 1,050			3.25	4.18	4.74

TABLE (contd.)

1,051 to 1,200	3.21	4.13	4.69
1,201 to 1,350	3.16	4.09	4.65
1,351 to 1,500	3.10	4.02	4.58
1,501 to 1,650	3.04	3.99	4.55
1,651 to 1,800	2.99	3.97	4.52
1,801 to 1,950	2.97	3.92	4.48
1,951 or more		3.90	4.46

13. Staff accommodation (1) Every school shall include a head teacher's room.

(2) In the case of a school –
    (a) with more than 250 pupils, or
    (b) attended by both boys and girls where the majority of pupils have attained the age of 11 years,
and, in the case of any special school, the school shall include a room for the senior assistant teacher.

(3) Every school shall include accommodation for use by the staff employed as teachers thereat, both for the purposes of work (otherwise than in teaching accommodation) and for social purposes.

Schedule 4

Teaching Accommodation

1. (1) This paragraph shall apply in the case of a nursery school or a school which includes one or more nursery classes, not being a special school.

(2) In the case of such a school there shall be teaching and playroom accommodation of a total minimum net area of $2.3m^2$ for each pupil at the nursery school or, as the case may be, in the nursery classes.

2. In the case of a school with one or more nursery classes the accommodation required by paragraph 1 shall be additional to that required by paragraph 3 or 4; but, for the purposes of paragraph 3 or 4, no account shall be taken of pupils in nursery classes.

3. (1) This paragraph shall apply in the case of any school which is neither a nursery school nor a special school.

(2) In the case of such a school there shall be a teaching accommodation of a total minimum net area which is the aggregate of the areas determined for each of the age groups specified in the following Table (subject to the following sub-paragraphs) in accordance with that Table by reference to –
    (a) the relevant total number of total pupils at the school, that is to say, the number of pupils who have not attained the age of 16 years or, in the case of a sixth form college, the number of pupils at the college, subject however to paragraph 2, and
    (b) the area for each pupil in the age group in question specified opposite the entry in the first column of the Table within which that relevant total number falls.

(3) Where the relevant total number of pupils at a school is 80 or less, the aggregate of the areas for the age groups specified in the second and third columns of the following Table, determined in accordance therewith, shall be increased by $70m^2$.

(4) In relation to the age group specified in the second column of the following Table (comprised by pupils who have not attained the age of 9 years), should –
    (a) the number of pupils in that age group exceed 600, or
    (b) though that number does not exceed 600, the relevant total number of pupils at the school exceed 700,
then, subject to reduction to take reasonable account of possible economies arising out of the numbers for whom teaching accommodation is provided ('economies of scale'), the area for each pupil in that age group shall be $2.19m^2$.

(5) In relation to the age group specified in the third column of the following Table (comprised by pupils who have attained the age of 9 but not that of 11 years), should the relevant total number of pupils at the school exceed 800 then, subject to reduction to take reasonable account of economies of scale, the area for each pupil in that age group shall be $2.31m^2$.

4. (1) This paragraph shall apply in the case of a special school.

(2) In the case of such a school there shall be teaching accommodation of a total minimum net area determined in accordance with the Table to paragraph 3 as hereinafter applied, that is to say, by reference to –
    (a) the relevant total number of pupils at the school, within the meaning of paragraph 3 (2) (a), and
    (b) the area for each pupil at the school (regardless of the age group into which he falls) specified in the final column of the Table opposite the entry in the first column within which that relevant total number falls.

Appendix B
Model Instrument and Articles of Government for a County Secondary School

Schedule to Administrative Memorandum No. 25 issued 26th
January, 1945

MINISTRY OF EDUCATION
EDUCATION ACT 1944

Models Instrument and Articles of Government for a County Secondary School

NOTES

I. The following suggestions are intended for the use of Local Education Authorities in drawing up Instruments and Articles of Government for County Secondary Schools. Authorities will find it generally convenient to include the Instrument and Articles in one document, but, inasmuch as the Instrument does not require the approval of the Minister of Education, it should be shown separately from the Articles in the manner indicated below.

II. Attention is directed to the Fourth Schedule to the Education Act, 1944, which contains additional provisions relating to meetings and proceedings of Governing Bodies.

III. Adequate representation should be given to women in the constitution of Governing Bodies and particularly in the case of Girls' and Mixed Schools.

IV. In accordance with the Interpretation Act, 1889, references to Headmaster and Master include also in appropriate cases Headmistress and Mistress.

V. In cases where several schools are grouped under one Governing Body it may be found convenient to set out the individual schools in a schedule both to the Instrument and Articles of Government. A separate Instrument and Articles must however be made for every School which is not grouped.

VI. Where a County Local Education Authority have made a Scheme of Divisional Administration it will be appreciated that some of the functions of the Local Education Authority under the Instrument and Articles of Government will be delegated to the Divisional Executive and, where this is the case, the true interpretation of the Instrument and Articles of Government will be obtained only when they are read in conjunction with that Scheme.

COUNTY [BOROUGH] COUNCIL
A. *INSTRUMENT OF GOVERNMENT*

The County (Borough) Council of
acting as the Local Education Authority hereby orders as follows:--

Governing Body
1. The Governing Body, hereinafter called "the Governors" of the
        School shall, when complete, consist of   persons, that
is to say:--
(   ) Representative Governors, to be appointed as follows:--
(   ) by the Local Education Authority
N.B. here add any other categories of Representative Governors
(   ) Co-optative Governors, to be appointed, except as hereinafter provided in the case of first such Governors, by resolution of the Governors.
The Representative Governors shall be appointed for a term of
        years; and thee Co-optative Governors, except as hereinafter provided, each for a term of   years.
A Representative Governor need not be a member of the appointing body.

First Governors and Meeting
2. (i) The following persons shall be deemed to be the first Co-optative Governors, and, subject to the provisions of this Instrument as to the termination of Governorship, shall be entitled to hold office for
        years.
N.B. Here insert names of first Co-optative Governors
    (ii) The First Representative Governors shall be appointed as soon as possible after the date of this Instrument, and their names shall be notified to the Clerk of the Governors on behalf of the Governors.
    (iii) The first meeting of the Governors under this Instrument shall be summoned by the said Clerk not later than the   day
of   1945, or, if he fails to summon a meeting for two months after that date, by any two Governors or by the Chief Education Officer.

Governors not to be financially Interested in the School
3. Except with the approval in writing of the Local Education Authority no Governor shall take or hold any interest in any property held or used for the purposes of the school or receive any

remuneration for his services, or be interested in the supply of work or goods to or for the purposes of the School.

Masters not to be Governors
4. No master or other person employed for the purposes of the School shall be a Governor.

Determination of Governorship
5. Any Governor who is absent from all meetings of the Governors during a period of one year, or who is adjudicated a bankrupt, or who is incapacitated from acting, or who communicates in writing to the Clerk of the Governors a wish to resign, shall thereupon cease to be a Governor.

Vacancies
6. Every vacancy in the office of Representative or Co-optative Governor shall as soon as possible be notified to the proper appointing body or person or filled by the Governors as the case requires. Any competent Governors may be re-appointed.

Casual Vacancies
7. A Governor appointed to fill a casual vacancy shall hold office only for the unexpired term of office of the Governor in whose place he is appointed.

Chairman
8. The Governors shall, at their first ordinary or stated meeting in each year, elect two of their number to be respectively Chairman and Vice-Chairman of their meetings for the year. If both the Chairman and the Vice-Chairman are absent from any meeting the members present shall choose one of their number to preside at that meeting before any other business is transacted. The Chairman and Vice-Chairman shall always be re-eligible.

Rescinding Resolutions
9. Any resolution of the Governors may be rescinded or varied at a subsequent meeting if due notice of the intention to rescind or vary the same has been given to all the Governors.

Adjournment of Meetings
10. If at the time appointed for a meeting a sufficient number of Governors to form a quorum is not present, or if at any meeting the business is not completed, the meeting shall stand ajourned sine-die, and a special meeting shall be summoned as soon as conveniently may be. Any meeting may be adjourned by resolution.

To be inserted in appropriate cases.

[*Application of Scheme of Divisional Administration*
11. Where the Local Education Authority have delegated under a Scheme of Divisional Administration to a Divisional Executive for the area in which the school is situated any of the powers and duties

of the Local Education Authority under this Instrument the expression "Local Education Authority" in this Instrument shall, where necessary, be deemed to refer to or to include, as the case may be, the Divisional Executive.]

Interpretation Act
12. The Interpretation Act, 1889, shall apply to the interpretation of this Instrument as it applies to an Act of Parliament.

Date of Instrument
13. The date of this Instrument shall be

B. ARTICLES OF GOVERNMENT

The County (Borough) Council of   acting as the Local Education Authority hereby orders as follows:–

Conduct of School
1. The   School shall be conducted in accordance with the provision of the Education Act, 1944, with the provisions of any Regulations made by the Minister of Education relating to County Secondary Schools and with these Articles.

Date of Articles
2. The date of these Articles shall be the 1st day of April, 1945, or the day on which the Minister of Education signifies his approval of these Articles, whichever is the later.

Finance
3. (a) The Governors shall in the month of   in each year submit for the consideration of the Local Education Authority an estimate of the income and expenditure required for the purposes of the school for the 12 months ending   in the following year, in such form as the Local Education Authority may require.

(b) The Local Education Authority shall consider the estimate and make such variations in it as they think fit.

(c) Where the Governors are empowered by the Local Education Authority to incur expenditure they shall not exceed the amount approved by the Local Education Authority under each head of the estimate in any year without the previous consent of the Local Education Authority.

School Premises
4. (a) The Governors shall from time to time inspect, and keep the Local Education Authority informed as to, the condition and state of repair of the school premises, and, where the Local Education Authority so permit, the Governors shall have power to carry out urgent repairs up to such an amount as may be approved by the Local Education Authority.

(b) The Governors shall, subject to any direction of the Local Education Authority, determine the use to which the school premises, or any part thereof, may be put out of school hours.

Appointment and Dismissal of Head Master

5. (a) The appointment and dismissal of the Headmaster shall conform to the following procedure:–

One or other of the alternatives to be inserted.

EITHER The vacant post shall be advertised by the Local Education Authority and a short list of three names shall be drawn up from the applications for the post by the Governors, a representative of the Local Education Authority being present. The final appointment shall be made by the Local Education Authority, a representative of the Governing Body being present.

OR The vacant post shall be advertised by the Local Education Authority and a short list shall be drawn up from the applications for the post by a Joint Committee consisting of an [equal number] of Governors and representatives of the Local Education Authority under the chairmanship of a person nominated by the Local Education Authority. The said Joint Committee shall also meet to interview the persons on the short list and shall recommend one person on the list for appointment by the Local Education Authority.

(b) The Head Master shall be employed under a contract of service in writing, determinable only (except in the case of dismissal for misconduct or any other urgent cause) upon [six/three] months written notice, taking effect at the end of a school term, which may be given by either side. Except when otherwise determined by the Local Education Authority he shall not be dismissed except on the recommendation of the Governors.

(c) A resolution of the governors to recommend the dismissal of the Headmaster shall not take effect until it has been confirmed at a meeting of the Governors, held not less than 14 days after the date of the meeting at which the resolution was passed. The Governors may by a resolution suspend for misconduct or any other urgent cause the Headmaster from his office pending the decision of the Local Education Authority.

(d) The Headmaster shall be entitled to appear, accompanied by a friend, at any meeting of the Governors or the Local Education Authority at which his dismissal is to be considered, and shall be given at least [three] days notice of such meeting.

Assistant Masters

6. The appointment and dismissal of assistant masters shall be subject to the following procedure:–

(a) On the occurence of a vacancy for an assistant master the Governors shall notify the Local Education Authority, who shall if they think fit, advertise the post and shall transmit to the Governors the names of candidates. Provided that the Local Education Authority may, if they think fit, and after giving full consideration to the views of the Governors and the Headmaster, require the Governors to appoint a master to be transferred from another school or from any pool of new entrants to the teaching profession.

(b) The appointment of assistant masters shall be made to the service of the Local Education Authority by the Governors in consultation with the Headmaster within the limits of the establishment of staff laid down for the current year by the Local Education Authority, and such appointments shall, except where made under the proviso to paragraph (a) of this Article, be subject to confirmation by the Local Education Authority.

(c) Appointments of assistant masters shall in all cases be determinable upon [   ] months notice in writing.

(d) The procedure for the dismissal or suspension of assistant masters shall be similar to that specified for Headmasters, except that two meetings of the Governors shall not be required.

Non-teaching Staff

7. (a) The non-teaching staff shall, subject to any general directions of the Local Education Authority, be appointed by the Governors, after consultations with the Head Master, to the service of the Authority and shall be dismissed by the Local Education Authority upon the recommendation of the Governors.

(b) The Clerk of the Governors shall be the Chief Education Officer or such other person as may be appointed by the Local Education Authority.

Organisation and Curriculum

8. (a) The Local Education Authority shall determine the general educational character of the school and its place in the local educational system. Subject thereto the Governors shall have the general direction of the conduct and curriculum of the school.

(b) Subject to the provisions of these Articles the Headmaster shall control the internal organisation, management and discipline of the school, shall exercise supervision over the teaching and non-teaching staff, and shall have the power of suspending pupils from attendance for any cause which he considers adequate but on suspending any pupil he shall forthwith report the case to the Governors, who shall consult the Local Education Authority.

(c) (i) There shall be a full consultation at all times between the Headmaster and the Chairman of the Governors.
(ii) All proposals and reports affecting the conduct and curriculum of the school shall be submitted formally to the Governors. [The Chief Education Officer or his representative shall be informed of such reports and proposals and be furnished with a copy thereof at least [7] days before they are considered]. _Sentence in square brackets to be omitted if circumstances make it unnecessary_
(iii) The Headmaster shall be entitled to attend through-out every meeting of the Governors, except on such occasions and for such times as the Governors may for good cause otherwise determine.
(iv) There shall be full consultation and co-operation between

the Headmaster and the Chief Education Officer on matters affecting the welfare of the school.

(v) Suitable arrangements shall be made for enabling the teaching staff to submit their views or proposals to the Governors through the Headmaster.

School Holidays

9. Holidays for the school shall be fixed by the Local Education Authority, but the Governors shall have power to grant mid-term or other occasional holidays not exceeding 10 days in any year.

Admission of Pupils

10. The admission of pupils to the school shall be in accordance with arrangements made by the Local Education Authority, which shall take into account the wishes of parents, any school records and other information which may be available, the general type of education most suitable for the particular child and the views of the Governors and the Headmaster as to the admission of the child to the School.

Returns

11. The Governors shall furnish to the Local Education Authority such returns and reports as the Authority may require.

Copies of Articles

12. A copy of these Articles shall be given to every Governor, the Headmaster, and every Assistant master on entry into office.

[*Application of Scheme of Divisional Administration*

To be inserted in appropriate cases. 13. Where the Local Education Authority have delegated under a Scheme of Divisional Administration to a Divisional Executive for the area in which the school is situated any of the powers and duties of the Local Education Authority under these Articles the expression "Local Education Authority" in these Articles shall, where necessary, be deemed to refer to or to include, as the case may be, the Divisional Executive.].

Interpretation Act

14. The Interpretation Act, 1889, shall apply to the interpretation of these Articles as it applies to an Act of Parliament.

Part 2:
Governors' Training Guide

Chapter 24

Introduction

The National Association of Governors and Managers has been asked on numerous occasions to organise training courses for governors. This guide is the result of our many attempts to do so, and will, we hope, help those who want to run such courses, and indeed groups of governors – or individuals – who feel they want help in doing the job more effectively.

It may perhaps elucidate our method if we explain how we originally set about the task of devising a course. A group of us (all governors of varying degrees of expertise) met originally in the summer of 1973 and after discussion decided that the questions we needed to ask were:

1. Who were our students? What characteristics did they share?
2. In what way did we want them to be different at the end of the course? What did we want them to be able to do?
3. How could we effect the change?

The answer to the first question threw up a fact of enormous importance to our whole approach – ie the total diversity of governors. Indeed, part of the point of governing bodies themselves is that they should represent all sectors of the community. We would have a student body, therefore, with a wide variety of educational and social backgrounds, and with a wide variety of degrees of experience in the education system and political system. The one thing which we decided they would probably have in common (not necessarily by virtue of their having been appointed as governors, but by virtue of their having decided to come on a course) was an interest in education and a desire to participate in the decisions to be made about it.

The answer to the second question was, we decided, in general terms this: at the end of the course, our students should be better acquainted with their powers and *how to use them* and with their duties and *how to fulfil them*. In order to be clear what we meant by this we listed the following skills we hoped our students might acquire:

1. The students should begin to get used to committee procedure and how to use it.
2. They should begin to understand how to define the needs of an individual school and how to go about seeing them answered.
3. They should learn to find their way about laws and regulations.
4. They should begin to explore their function as a link between the school and the community.
5. They should learn how to keep a watchful eye on the bureaucracy of

the education service.

6. They should learn how to ask constructive questions about the 'conduct and curriculum' of the school, which it is their duty to oversee, without appearing to interfere in the 'internal management' which is the head's responsibility.

7. They should learn how and when to translate discussion into action.

This brought us (by this time at a subsequent meeting) to a consideration of the crucial third question: how to do it? It seemed clear to us that the only possible way to learn all these things was by doing them, and that therefore the linch-pin of our course must be actually practising going through governors' meetings. We hoped that the desire to participate which we premised as a common characteristic in our students would ensure their willingness to learn in this way, and that their diversity of experience, rather than being a problem, would be turned to maximum advantage in enabling them to learn from each other. In both these hopes we have been fully justified on every occasion we have run the course.

We then proceeded to construct a number of 'simulated agendas' of governing body meetings of imaginary schools, dealing with the usual matters that arise – accommodation problems, finance, an appointment, a suspension, and so on. These agendas we used in May 1974, and subsequently on a number of courses. The agendas are produced on page 119. (However, we do now feel that actual agendas from the authority where the course is being run will be more effective. This is more fully discussed later.)

From the beginning we asked our students for comment and criticism on the course, and have amended it in the light of these. One comment from the start was that, however effective the simulation technique might be for learning how to do things, there was still a need for a handy reference book of vital information about the education system, which governors need before they even start. Some authorities do produce such a handbook, but not by any means at all. In order to meet this need we produced the *School Governors' Handbook* which forms the greater part of this book and which should, we hope, be a useful introduction for all governors as well as being essential reading for the participants of any course being run on the lines we suggest.

Another criticism we have tried to meet is that a course consisting largely of simulated meetings could overemphasise the importance of the actual meetings, and leave out of consideration the importance of informal contacts between governors and the schools they govern. We have therefore included discussion and advice on this sort of activity in the *Handbook*.

We have also learnt from experience that there is an important place in a course of this sort for the more conventional lecture or 'question and answer' session with education officers, inspectors etc. Questions are bound to be thrown up by the simulation sessions that cannot be fully explored in that context, and we have found it useful to collect these questions until near the end of the course and then present a speaker or panel of speakers who can answer them authoritatively. We feel, however, that such a session must come at the end, when the participants have developed a degree of confidence in their own competence. It is also useful to realise in advance that 'role-playing' can be fairly exhausting, and if the course is an intensive one (like, for instance, one we ran morning and afternoon for a week) it helps to break up the simulation sessions with lectures and discussions. The basic method of the course can be adapted to almost any form and time-span, and we make suggestions about the possible different arrangements on page 112.

The most important modification of our original intention in putting the course together arises from our realisation of the limitations of our materials. Some problems that arise in governing bodies are perennial, and those that use the simulated agendas in this book will probably recognise them, but a great many are topical to a particular area at a particular date, and our original simulated agendas contained too many of the problems peculiar to inner-urban areas in the period 1973–74 (although we have subsequently amended them to some extent) to be entirely appropriate for use in all authorities at all times. In addition, government regulations and economic constraints are constantly changing. We now feel, therefore, that each course for governors should have its own agendas, preferably actual ones from meetings held within the previous year in that LEA. Names and other details by which the school can be identified can be removed and even some items changed to keep its anonymity more secure – and perhaps other items added so as to cover all issues; but a basis of this sort in the reality of the local situation is likely, we feel, to provide a more useful learning situation than the examples we provide in this book. Individual items, however, from our agendas could easily be 'lifted' and used in combination with actual local ones.

The following pages therefore contain: possible programmes of courses based on the use of simulated governors' meetings; a section on how to run a simulation session with either our own or other agendas; and finally, our own model agendas. In Appendix C are examples of the sort of questions we would expect to be raised on one of the agendas.

Chapter 25

Possible Programmes

Authorities and institutions that run courses for governors usually do so on the basis of a series (up to six) of two-hour weekly sessions, either in the morning or in the evening, or of a single-day conference. We have used the simulated agendas as a basis for both, and also for a week-long intensive course. Programmes for all three ways of doing it are outlined below. The material has also been used with students on a Post-Graduate Certificate of Education course, as a way of 'kicking off' a unit on the education system.

The maximum number for a simulation session is 30, the minimum number about 10. A course that has more than 30 students will therefore have to be sub-divided for those parts of it that are simulation sessions. The only limitation on total numbers would be (a) the capacity of the hall or large room for plenary sessions (if these are wanted), and (b) the available staffing (two per simulation session – or in some circumstances, one – see the first paragraph of Chapter 26 on How to Run a Simulation Session).

Day Conference

Morning:	Brief introduction.
	Simulation session, with a break for coffee, with a choice of agendas, if the numbers warrant it: primary school governors' meeting, appointment, secondary school governors' meeting, suspensions etc.
Afternoon:	Discussion in groups *not* the same as the morning groups, of questions that have arisen during the morning sessions. (Instructors would have to discuss and compile these over lunch.)
	Tea.
	Panel of 'experts': education officer, councillor, head or teacher to answer questions in a plenary session.

Course of Six Weekly Sessions

1. Primary agenda, containing matters of rolls and accommodation and school activities.
2. Primary agenda, containing matters of staffing and finance.
3. Appointment meeting (see note on our model appointment meeting).
4. Secondary meeting, containing a report on curriculum, examination

results and distribution of Burnham Scale points.
5. Secondary meeting, containing a report on school rules, discipline and an appeal against suspension.
6. Questions to an invited panel on issues that have arisen during the five simulation sessions.

Week-long Intensive Course

Day 1. *Morning:* Primary agenda, containing matters of rolls and accommodation and school activities.

Afternoon: Talk and/or discussion on LEA's and governors' responsibilities for school sites, buildings, admission policies. (References: Education Acts, Instrument and Articles of Government Regulations for school premises.)*

Day 2. *Morning:* Primary agenda, containing matters of staffing and finance.

Afternoon: Lecture on distribution of responsibility for finance.*

Day 3. *Morning:* Appointment meeting.

Afternoon: Students to prepare and discuss questions that should have been asked (but were not) of the candidates in the morning session. Further discussion of how appointment procedures could be improved.

Day 4. *Morning:* Secondary meeting, including discussion of curriculum and examination results.

Afternoon: Seminar on new sorts of curriculum development and examination courses, and the proper function of governors in relation to these.*

Day 5. *Morning:* Secondary meeting, including distribution of Burnham Scale points, and an appeal against suspension.

Afternoon: Discussion on the role of governors in liaison with other sections of the community.

These sessions marked * might benefit from an outside expert.

Chapter 26

How to Run a Simulation Session

Preparation

The first thing to do is to make sure the number attending, the rooms available, and the personnel at your disposal all match up. There should be not more than 30 and not less than 10 students to each group; each group must have a room big enough to be arranged for a governors' meeting, with chairs around a table if possible, and an outer ring of chairs if there are more than 15 students. To run each group you need two people (one of whom will be the instructor) with a reasonable knowledge of the education system and some experience of a governing body, to play the roles of head and clerk. We have asked all sorts of people to do this, many of them people who are in no sense professional educators, and have found that although some experience on a governing body is essential, alertness and readiness to improvise are more important than expert knowledge. If you have an opportunity to get to know the group with whom you are running a simulation exercise, you may be able to pick out one of the students who could play one of the roles.

The next job is to assemble the agenda and papers. This can take time and it is wise to start at least a month before the course is due to start. As we explained in the Introduction, we feel that the most useful model is a local one. You should approach your local education authority and ask if you may have an actual agenda, with head's report, to work from, explaining that you would of course expect all names to be blocked out to preserve the school's anonymity. If the local authority feels unable to supply you with these, you must then try to persuade someone to concoct an agenda with head's report based on local experience. The people most likely to do this well are heads or experienced governors: they may feel able to lift and disguise parts out of their own meetings and papers. The areas you will want covered include the school roll, accommodation, teaching staff, finance, academic results, discipline problems – in fact the subjects covered by many of the chapters in the *Handbook*.

The papers relating to the meeting should be in three parts: the agenda, or order of business; the written head's report (which is one item on the agenda and should be taken early); and any background material that is supplied by the authority to explain particular items on the agenda – this may be an explanation of the salary scales, directions about fire precautions, details of procedures for appointments, suspensions etc. These papers are not strictly necessary, and indeed if you are only running a single simulation session will probably be superfluous, but they can be a very useful way of introducing background knowledge of how the system works, and also of encouraging students to read what they are sent by the authority in a critical and enquiring spirit – papers of this sort sometimes have a bureaucratic tendency to confuse rather than enlighten. Local authorities that are unwilling to allow you to use particular governing bodies' agenda papers may very well be happy to supply you with copies of this type of circular to governors and when you are asking for papers in the beginning you should ask for them separately.

You should also ask for copies of the Instrument and Articles of Government and the relevant documents for voluntary schools too if there are likely to be voluntary school governors on the course. Your students, if they are already governors, should have these documents and should be asked to bring them with them. (If they have not been supplied with them, they should be encouraged to write to the Education Office and ask for them.) These documents should be kept for reference in any discussion that arises as to the rules of procedure and the precise nature of the duties and responsibilities of governing bodies.

If possible, the papers for the simulated meeting should be circulated to all the participants several days beforehand, with an explanation if necessary that they will be expected to act as if they were in fact governors of the school in question. If you concoct your own agenda, you can include a 'description of the school' (as we have done, see page 122) which we have found helps students to get involved in the simulation.* If you are using a real agenda, it is more difficult to do this in view of the need to preserve anonymity.

The last piece of preparation needed is a meeting between the 'head' and 'clerk' to go through the agenda and head's report and decide how they are going to 'play' it, and agree any background 'story' that may be necessary so that the school and its problems as they appear present a reasonably consistent picture. This preparation can never preclude the need to improvise as the simulation proceeds, however. It should be stressed that this will not need any dramatic talent at all. The material will probably be full enough for the roles to 'play themselves'. However, the clerk and head can, if they choose, plan to be deliberately obstructive or vague or stupid or overbearing, or, on the other hand briskly competent and confident – whichever appears to them will be most instructive for their students.

Layout and Timing

The room should be laid out as described above – with a large table (or desks arranged as a large table) in the middle, and chairs around it. If there are more than 15 students, then the group should be divided in two, with half seated around the table as the 'governors', and the other half in a circle behind them as audience and critics.

The instructor should start by explaining briefly that they are all (or the inner ring first) going to pretend to be the governors of the school for which they have already seen the papers; that while they are playing a role they should try to stay in role, but that there will be frequent breaks for discussion and questions. He should then introduce himself as the clerk, appointed by

---

* Alternatively you can, as we have done with the secondary school agenda (Training Agenda No 3), create a 'prospectus' for the school, in other words a document which describes the school as it wishes to project itself.

the authority, and introduce the head teacher (or the other way round, if that is what has been decided). He should call the meeting to order and ask for nominations for chairman.

This is a valuable way of putting the initiative immediately with the students, and usually produces a suggestion even from a group of disparate people largely unknown to each other. However, if there is no nomination from the 'governors', the instructor can ask someone to take the chair to begin with. After the first session there should be no problem in getting nominations. It is probably a good idea to ask for a new chairman each time, and at some stage in the course to discuss what makes a good and bad chairman (with self-critical examples drawn from the performances of the participants). If the session is in two groups alternating as participants and audience, then of course the chairman should change too.

If the group are very inexperienced, the instructor may feel that he needs to select a chairman; on the whole, however, we feel this is better avoided. The group can learn a lot about meetings by trying to cope with a not altogether competent chairman. Once the chairman is appointed the clerk should as far as possible leave the management of the meeting to him, except for the decision when to break for discussion and self-criticism. This can be done after each item on the agenda, but sometimes it is better to let the 'meeting' proceed for a longer time – say up to half an hour – so that the participants get into their stride. If half the group is acting as 'audience', one of these breaks should be used as an opportunity to change the groups over.

The questions to be asked during these breaks for self-criticism are: 'Have we understood what was needed here? What have we achieved? Have we taken the action that was necessary, in the form of a resolution or a request for information? Have we left any loose ends?' and so on. The insights gained by these periods of analysis should enable the group to perform more effectively when they return to their roles. If the group is in two halves it is generally more encouraging to allow each half at least two tries – ie to give them the opportunity to show how they have benefited from criticism – before the other half take their places.

Near the beginning of most agendas are standard items: Minutes, Matters Arising, Action Taken. In a single-session simulation, these will be dispensed with, but if the agenda is being run over several meetings it is a useful exercise to construct these items after one meeting, based on what occurred, and then take them at the beginning of the next. Again, the minutes can be inaccurate or incomplete, and the action taken inadequate or presumptuous, so as to alert the students to the importance of keeping an eye on these items.

In timing the session, the instructor should bear in mind whether it is a single session or one of a series. If it is a single session he will want to make sure everybody gets a chance to participate and that a reasonable amount of business is done; therefore prolonged discussion should be avoided. If the course consists of a number of simulation sessions, then he could allow two or even three 'meetings' in which to cover the agenda.

It is possible to delegate certain students on the course to be the teacher governor, the parent governor, the local councillor, and so on. This would be particularly feasible if the students do not start the first session of the course with a simulated meeting, but have a talk or a discussion first, and an opportunity to discuss the different roles. However, in the experience of those who have acted as instructors in the past, jumping straight into the simulation is in fact the best way of ensuring maximum participation, and too much 'scene setting' by allocating different parts distracts attention from the main purpose of the sessions which is to learn how to be an effective manager or governor, not to take part in a charade. Of course, the students themselves may feel the need to have a representative of parents, teachers, etc present, and if the idea comes from them, then it should be acted on.

For the first Training Agenda that follows we have given examples, in Appendix C, of the sort of questions that we would expect alert governors to raise under different items and the sort of action we would expect them to take. The instructor should run through the agenda and head's report before the session and formulate some ideas about what ought to be discussed and done in the situation of this imaginary school. However, he may find a rather different picture emerging from the questions and improvised answers that result, and he has to be ready for that too. It is an exercise in which the instructor has to think and respond quickly, go with the mood and interests of the group, but keep the basic object well in view. In fact it is an exercise, for the instructor, in just those 'committee skills' which it is part of his object to impart to the students. Perhaps this is one of the reasons for the success we feel the method enjoys.

The NAGM's Training Agendas

TRAINING AGENDA NO 1

Instructor's Note

The first Training Agenda is the governors' meeting of an ordinary county primary school. There is enough business to last for two or three sessions, with breaks for discussion and criticism. One session will probably only just get through item 2, Head's Report, but enough issues are covered in this to make it a worthwhile exercise on its own.

This is the simplest and least technical agenda, and therefore the best to begin with on a long course. Possible questions that might be expected to arise under each item are listed in Appendix C as an aid to instructors.

TRAINING AGENDA NO 1

Papers to be Distributed to Students

REGAL LANE JUNIOR MIXED AND INFANTS SCHOOL

Inspector's Confidential Inter-Office Memo Describing the School*

Regal Lane Primary School was built in 1882, a typical Victorian backstreet school. it is now designated as 'JM & I' (Junior Mixed and Infants). Outwardly it is gaunt and prison-like, but inside a fairly imaginative use of the high, light classrooms and wide corridors give it a cheerful atmosphere.

The accommodation consists of a hall (which doubles as a dining-room), seven classrooms, a library, a small staff room, head's room cum office, stock room (converted cloakrooms, coats hang in the corridors), two internal lavatories and ten outside lavatories.

There is an unrelieved asphalt playground. The total site area is one acre.

The neighbourhood is socially mixed, but in what estate agents would call a 'desirable area' of the inner city. Ten years ago it was largely occupied by working-class unfurnished tenants, with one smallish pre-war coucil block, and one or two very attractive early nineteenth-century terraces beginning to be occupied by professional middle-class families. In the last two years the district has polarised; more of it has become middle-class owner-occupied, and more of it has become run down. A number of properties have been bought up by the council and are 'awaiting development'. Meanwhile they are partly empty and subject to vandals; some are occupied by squatters, some have been taken over by the local council for the temporary housing of families in urgent housing need.

The school itself is run in a fairly middle-of-the-road, laissez-faire

---

* *Note:* such a confidential memo would not normally be seen by the governors of a school. It is included here to compensate for the fact that the 'governors' can have no first-hand experience of Regal Lane. To some extent they will be better informed therefore than their counterparts in real life.

way (some 'progressive' and some 'traditional' teachers, each following her own bent in her own classroom) by a head who has been in the job for ten years and is pleasant and well-intentioned but by now a little tired. He is also overpowered by a formidable deputy who rather assertively dominates the teaching of music and drama in the school (using a good proportion of the school's resources for this) but is not a great deal of help in the administration.

The school is well supported by local parents. A PTA was established by the head nine years ago and operates cheerfully though in a fairly conventional way (jumble sales, etc).

Over the last few years the school has gradually become more popular, partly because of its increasing percentage of middle-class children, and although there is not a shortage of school places over the wider area, this particular school is becoming overcrowded. Some children are coming in from outside the immediate neighbourhood (the LEA has no 'catchment area' policy); and there is now the added problem of sudden increased demand from within the neighbourhood because of the council's decision to put in 'urgent need' housing cases on a temporary basis.

REGAL LANE JUNIOR MIXED AND INFANTS SCHOOL

Governors' Meeting to be Held at the School on 8 October

AGENDA

1.   Election of Chairman

2.   Head's report (a) Rolls and Accommodation
                     (b) Teaching Staff
                     (c) Improvements
                     (d) Other Reports

3.   School Allowance. The headmaster's proposals for expenditure of the capitation allowance for the coming year are as follows:

Allowance notified by the Education Officer   £5,060

Proposed expenditure:
    Apparatus, consumable material, etc   3,000
    Books (other than library)   1,800
    Library   360
    Activities and Amenities   200
    Prizes   100
    Major Equipment   600
                                             £5,060

4.   Nursery Class. Proposals for the establishment of a nursery class to be built on the school playground. Plans are attached.

5.   Visiting Governors

6.   Date of next meeting

7.   Other urgent business

HEAD'S REPORT (Agenda Item 2)

(a) Rolls and Accommodation

The school roll has continued to rise, and there are now 220 children on roll. This is a very high figure considering that it is only October, and we would normally expect another intake of statutory 5's in January. Several of our classes now have over 30 children, and in some years I am having to turn away children. This has happened with a number of the children who have moved in, in the last two weeks, into the terrace of houses across the road which are being used as a temporary housing by the Borough Housing Department. The number of families in these houses seems to be rising as does the number of 'squatter' families in the district.

The school is beginning to feel very congested. At the moment the library is used in the mornings for remedial teaching and is only available for the school's use in the afternoon. Unless remedial teaching is moved into the hall (in which case it well have to stop at 11.45 when the kitchen staff insist they have to start setting out dinner tables), and an eighth class, taught by my deputy, takes the library, I do not know how the pressure is to be relieved. If this course is adopted not only will the library be lost to the rest of the school but all the very good work in music which the deputy head gives so much time to, will suffer.

(b) Teaching Staff

I was asked last term to prepare a list of the staff, with their length of service and special responsibilities. There has been considerable change since then, and here is the up-to-date list:

Full-Time	No of Years in School	Scale Posts
Mrs Smith (Deputy)	13	Deputy
Mrs Power	5	Scale 3 Responsibility for Reception arrangements, Infants. Liaison with local playgroups.
Miss James	3	Reading throughout the school. Scale 2.
Mr Wright	20	Scale 2. Boys' games.
Mrs Howard	1	
Mrs Carruthers	Probationer	
Miss Aaron	Probationer	
Mr Rowland	Probationer	

Part-Time

Mrs Gregory	.5	Remedial
Mr George	.2	Brass band

As the governors will see, we have three probationers this year. They have all settled well, particularly Mr Rowland who is an understanding young teacher. He came to us on teaching practice and we were lucky enough to be able to persuade him to return to the full-time staff.

The Education Office have notified me that under Burnham arrangements the school has one more scale point to use. I am recommending to the governors that we should offer it to Mrs Howard, who is in fact the only teacher eligible for it. She came as a probationer last year, and has settled in well. She is particularly interested in art and needlework, and I recommend that her post should be for art and craft throughout the school.

Mr George, the teacher of brass instruments, is a newcomer to the school. Mrs Smith was anxious to have some brass instruments in the little orchestra that she is getting together. As you know she teaches the string instruments and the recorder herself. She would also like a teacher for woodwind, but it is hard to find one. As the governors know, the school won second prize in the music festival last term; there are several very musical children in the school, and it is a pity not to have the full range of instruments for them.

(c) School Meals

About 200 children stay for school dinners; the rest go home. 31 children have free dinners.

The eating arrangments and the quality of the food are satisfactory. However, we have suffered this term from a shortage of kitchen staff, and this has meant that the teachers have sometimes had to help clear the hall so that it can be ready for music or PE in the afternoon.

We are also disturbed by the amount of food that is wasted by the children. We don't any more believe in making children eat, but we worry sometimes that some of them are not getting enough to sustain them through the day.

(d) Improvements

I have to report that the shelves promised for the staff room have not yet arrived. The display boarding for the library has arrived, but has not yet been fixed. It is stacked against one wall of the library, and has been there for several weeks, waiting for the man to come and fix it.

I have been informed by the office that the installation of sinks in the four upstairs classrooms, which we were promised two years ago, has been deferred yet again because of the reduction in the authority's minor works budget. This makes painting and modelling and any sort of messy work in those classrooms a nightmare to organise, particularly with the large classes we have at present.

(e) Other Reports

Transfer   27 children left us last term to go to secondary
school. Of these:
15 went to New Park Mixed Comprehensive
3 went to St Mary's Covent
4 went to John Brown Boys' Comprehensive
2 went to private schools
2 moved out of the district
1 went to Ashton School for children with
behavioural difficulties

School Journey   All these children, except three, went on the school journey to North Wales, where they explored and studied local history. They have prepared an account of their holiday which the governors may be interested in seeing.

Confidential   I am sorry to have to tell managers of some trouble with a pupil whom I will call John. I do not normally trouble governors with things of this sort, but there has been a lot of local gossip about this case, and I think it is best that the governors should know the whole story. The boy came to us last term and has been something of a problem from the start, inclined to be aggressive and start fights in the playground. There was some trouble in the summer between a shopkeeper in Ridge Road, and a group of boys including John. The shopkeeper suspected the boys of pilfering, and we never got to the bottom of it. On September 10th, John slipped out at playtime and stole a small transistor radio. The police were called and came round straight away to see me. I found John in his classroom with the radio in his pocket. Unfortunately, all the children knew the whole story, and having the police in and discovering the stolen goods actually on the premises created a very unhealthy atmosphere. However, John seems to have been given a fright by the incident; he is very subdued at the moment and we are keeping a careful eye on him.

John lives in the terrace of 'half-way houses' I described earlier, and he is not the only child from there who is showing signs of stress. Not only are many of the families somewhat unstable, but they are not very well received by some sections of the rest of the community, and a certain amount of tension is developing. Apparently the council is intending to use more of its recently acquired property in this area in the same way, and I can foresee problems for the school if they do.

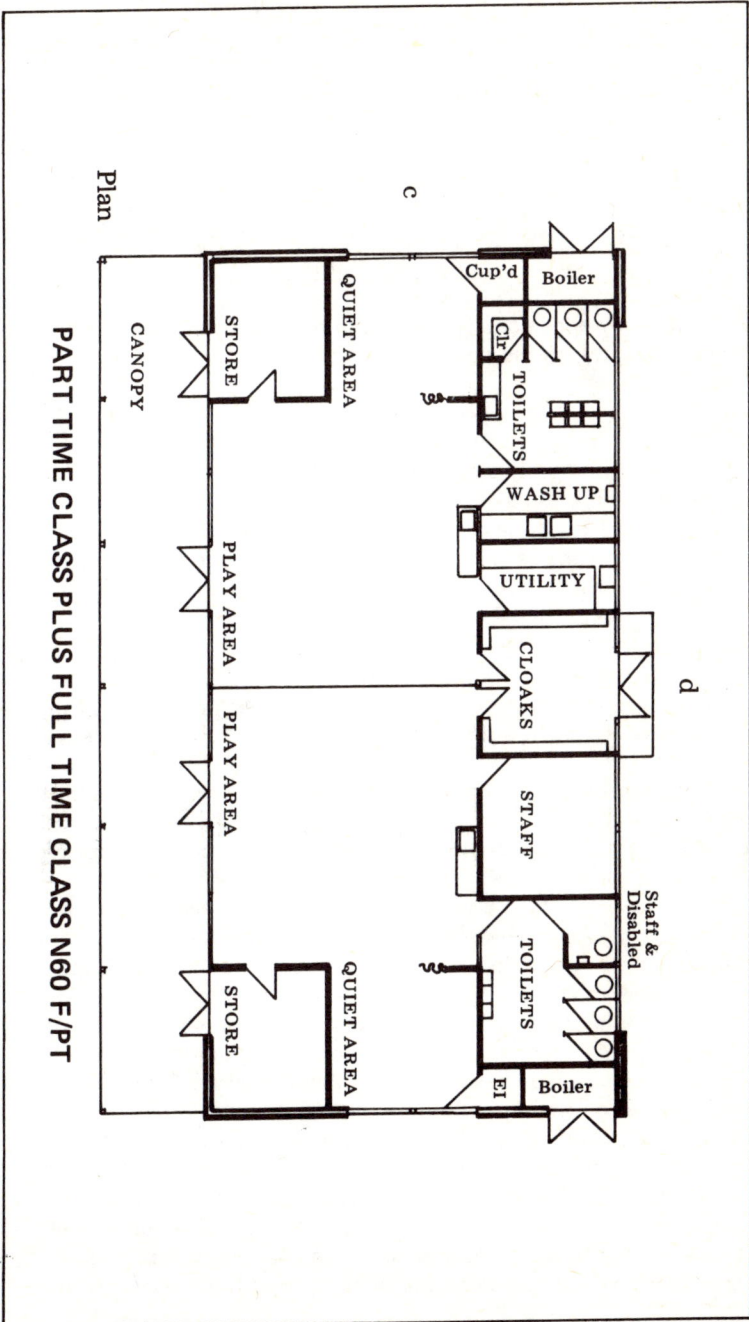

PART TIME CLASS PLUS FULL TIME CLASS N60 F/PT

Plan

c

d

CANOPY

STORE

QUIET AREA

PLAY AREA

PLAY AREA

QUIET AREA

STORE

Cup'd

Boiler

Clr

TOILETS

WASH UP

UTILITY

CLOAKS

STAFF

Staff & Disabled

TOILETS

EI

Boiler

TRAINING AGENDA NO 2

Instructor's Note

APPOINTMENT OF A DEPUTY HEAD TO REGAL LANE PRIMARY SCHOOL

(The vacancy arises out of the appointment of Mrs Smith, the present deputy, to the post of music adviser to another authority)

Note to Instructor:

This meeting is rather differently conducted, and it is not appropriate here to have two groups. However, there are more specific parts to be played, and it may be that when these have been allocated the remaining group is not too large to be a single governing body. If it is, then some students will have to be only audience/critics.

It is likely that there will not be enough time at the end of the session for a proper discussion of the performance; if this is the case, time should be made to complete it at the following session.

Personnel for this session needs consideration. There should be the clerk, head teacher, local authority adviser and the three candidates. Of these the most important are the candidates. Unless they can give a moderately knowledgeable performance, in accordance with the character sketch they have been given, the governors may not be given a chance to try out their skills of questioning and decision-making. It is usually possible to select three students who would be capable of doing this; in our exerience it is better to handpick them than to ask for volunteers. If you feel that there are not any, or enough, suitable people in the group, then you may have to import them. Real teachers, or experienced governors, would be useful. The part of the clerk in this agenda is purely mechanical, and therefore the instructor could delegate this to someone less experienced, and take on the head's or adviser's role. The adviser is included mainly for verisimilitude. A senior appointment of this sort would not be made without one! However, the learning experience of the students will be the greater if he does not do all the work, or lead the discussion too obviously, and if you cannot find anyone to take the part, you can invent an explanation for his sudden inability to attend and proceed without him. In reality this would be a loss: in the simulation it just gives the student more work to do.

Preparation

The students should have been given the description of Regal Lane Primary School and should have already worked through at least part of the agenda. They should also be reminded to read Chapter 8 on Appointments in the Handbook.

They should have been given time, before this meeting, to read through all the applications.

The three 'candidates' should be given the character sketch relevant to the character each is playing well before the meeting (Appendix D), but nobody else should see these at this stage. These are meant to give the 'true story' behind the application forms and confidential reports.

Procedure

The 'candidates' should be asked to leave the room. The clerk should ask for nominations for chairman. The chairman should then be left to conduct the meeting, unless he goes badly wrong, in which case the clerk or the adviser could remind him of the normal procedure, which is:

1.   A discussion of the job and its requirements (based on the needs of the school as it has been seen at the previous meetings); with some conclusions about the sort of questions which will be useful. (See below – Discussion.)
2.   Interview of candidates in turn, with the chairman opening the questioning, followed by other governors, head, inspector.
3.   The 'confidential' on each candidate read after each interview, but no discussion to take place until the end.
4.   Summing up of candidates by adviser or head.
5.   Discussion and decision by governors.

All this can be played 'in role' without a break, or the instructor can break for criticism at one or more points.

After the decision, the character sketches should be circulated to all students, and they should be asked to consider what aspects their questioning failed to uncover and what difference it would have made.

There should also be discussion and criticism of the way in which governors treated all the applicants both during the interview and when their decisions were announced.

Discussion

Either before the interview starts, or subsequently, it may be useful to have a more general discussion of appointment procedures. This might cover the following points:

Recruitment

- Who has responsibility for formulating the job analysis (what is done, how it is done and why it is done) and subsequently the job description?
- Would it be helpful to write a person specification for the job?
- Would it be helpful to use the original National Institute of Industrial Psychology 'seven point plan' to check characteristics necessary for the job?
  a) Physical characteristics
  b) Attainment
  c) General intelligence
  d) Special aptitudes
  e) Interests
  f) Personality
  g) Circumstances

Advertising

- Who decides on the wording of the advertisement for the vacant post?
- Where will the advertisement be placed?
- Who decides where the advertisement will be placed?

Selection

- Who can and wants to be involved in any shortlisting?
- Who can and wants to be involved in the interviewing?
- When and where should the interviewing take place?
- Should questions to the candidate be decided before the interview?
- If there is a job analysis and job description, should questions be tied in with them?

- If the 'seven point plan' is used should questions be tied in with that?
- Should it be decided beforehand who will ask the questions and in what order?
- What professional support will be available during the meeting, ie Inspector/Adviser?
- Do governors have the final choice of the deputy or does it rest with the LEA?

Equal Opportunities

- What is the policy of the Authority in respect of equal opportunities? What guidance do the governors need to fulfil their duties in this respect?

Note: Simply for the purpose of working out the ages and past experience of the candidates, the appointment meeting should be assumed to be taking place in October 1985.

TRAINING AGENDA NO 2

(including Appendix D at end of session)

Papers to be Distributed to Students

REGAL LANE PRIMARY SCHOOL

Governors are invited to attend a meeting for the appointment to the post of Deputy Head.

The following advertisement has appeared, and details of three shortlisted candidates are enclosed.

Regal Lane (JM & I) Applications are invited from experienced teachers for the post of Deputy Head Teacher (Group 4), required as soon as possible. Candidates should have good organising ability and capacity to lead a young and enthusiastic staff. Vacancy due to promotion.

CONFIDENTIAL

Details of candidates

MISS FRANCES HOLMES   AGE: 27

Present address: 1, Surrey Lane, Saddleton*

Education and Training:
1969–76 St George's Girls School, Saddleton
1976–79 Somerville College, Oxford
1979–80 Oxford School of Education

Qualifications:
1979 BA (Hons) 1st class (English Literature)
1980 Post Graduate Certificate in Education (with distinction)

Teaching Experience:
1980–82 Assistant teacher (assigned after 1st year) Lee School
(Junior)
1982 to date, Scale 2, Lee School

Supporting statement: 'Since qualifying I have taught at Lee Junior
School, and have gained there experience of Inner City children and
their parents. I have taught children of very varied social and racial
backgrounds and have come to believe that the difficulties involved
in this are more than compensated for by the educational value and
intellectual stimulus that this heterogeneity can bring. Over the last
four years I have developed my main interest in educational visits
and project work (for which I hold a Scale 2 post) and have found
that its value in arousing interest and sustaining concentration is
very great. I try to link both reading and number work with these
projects and my class's work on 'Birds of London' was exhibited at
a national conference last year. I have been responsible for
arranging educational visits for the whole school and have taken
trouble to arrange a large number of appropriate visits for each
class.

'I also enjoy music, play the cello, and have written a short opera
with my class which was performed to the parents last term.

* This town is 45 minutes' train journey away from the area in which Regal Lane School is situated,
but her present job is at a school in the same district as Regal Lane.

As I am a class teacher, I do not feel that I could make myself available until next September.'

MRS MARY POWER

AGE: 44

<u>Present address:</u> 15 Regal Avenue*

<u>Education and Training:</u>
1952–54 Whitely End Boarding School for the Daughters of Clergymen, Derbyshire
1960–63 St Mark's Training College, Sussex

<u>Qualifications:</u>
1963 Teacher's Certificate

<u>Teaching Experience:</u>
1963–66 Assistant teacher at Sandhill Infants School, Worthing
1978–79 Assigned Regal Lane JM & I
1979–82 Scale 2, Regal Lane
1982 to date, Scale 3, Regal Lane

<u>Other Experience:</u>
1957–60 With British Red Cross in Europe
1969–74 Member and later Vice-Chairman of Campaign for Children in Hospital
1973–77 Committee member of local Playgroup Association
1975–79 Chairman of Grange Primary School PTA

<u>Supporting Statement:</u> 'I have lived for eighteen years in this part of the city and feel that I know the area and its community well. As a parent I have been active in several local organisations and believe very strongly that links between home and schools are of increasing importance.

'I have taught at this school for five years and for the last four have held a special responsiblity post for reception arrangements and have enjoyed this part of my work very much, particularly the contact it brings with playgroups and families in the neighbourhood. I would be very happy to continue serving the school in the capacity of Deputy Head.'

* This address is three minutes' walk from the school.

MR IAN WALTON   AGE: 29

<u>Present address:</u> 18, North Street, Frog's Hill*

<u>Education and Training:</u>
1968–75 South London Boys' Grammar School
1975–78 St Wilfred's College of Education Bristol

<u>Qualifications:</u>
1980 Teacher's Diploma

<u>Teaching Experience:</u>
1980–81 Divisional staff, teaching at Uland School
1981–83 Assigned, Scale 2, St John's Junior School
1983 to date Assigned, Scale 3, Rodway Junior School

<u>Supporting Statement:</u> 'My teaching career has been in three very different schools and I feel that I have developed from this experience the sort of organisational skills and understanding that are needed for the job of deputy head.

'In my present job I am responsible for an annexe a quarter of a mile from the main school containing five classrooms, and am therefore used to exercising responsibility on my own. I have done my best in this situation to keep the children in touch with the main school, which is necessary so that they feel some continuity in their education, without at the same time overburdening the young and inexperienced teachers under me with too many journeys to supervise between the two buildings.

'I have also had responsibility for sport. I have organised Saturday football and have also trained the senior boys for athletics competitions. I find this an excellent way of getting to know some of the more difficult children, whom I have particularly tried to help.'

---

* This area is about 20 minutes' walk, five minutes' car journey, from the school. His present school is in a neighbouring authority's area.

CONFIDENTIAL REPORTS

to be read by the clerk

FRANCES HOLMES

Miss Holmes is an outstanding young teacher of strong character who has shown herself capable of bringing out the very best in her pupils and in stimulating their interest in a range of topics. During the time she has held her Scale Posts for educational visits the work of her school has been among the liveliest in London. Her relationship with the children is excellent and most of her colleagues recognise her ability and are prepared to follow her lead. Although she is young, and only has experience of one school, I feel I can recommend her for this post.

DISTRICT INSPECTOR

MARY POWER

During the five years Mrs Power has been teaching at Regal Lane she has shown herself to be a competent teacher, and a soothing and mature influence on younger teachers. She has good relations with parents and with many people in the neighbourhood, which she knows well. I am sure that she would be a suitable appointment as Deputy Head.

DISTRICT INSPECTOR

IAN WALTON

Mr Walton has show himself an efficient organiser and a natural administrator during the two years he has been a teacher at this school. His relations with staff and children are very good, and he has been successful in managing the annexe – at times very much on his own, as both my deputy and I have been on sick leave this year. I will be very sorry to lose him, but can recommend him highly.

HEAD OF RODWAY SCHOOL

TRAINING AGENDA NO 3

Instructor's Note

There is enough material in this agenda for two or even three sessions. If it is being run in one session, it would be wise for the instructor to select those items of the head's report he feels would be most useful for his students and omit the rest.

This agenda presents a considerable amount of information about the school, all of which will provoke questions of detail which the instructor will have to improvise answers for. It is therefore particularly important for the 'clerk' and 'head' to meet beforehand and fill out as consistent a picture of John Milton as possible after a close reading of the papers.

The 'governors' here are faced with a more challenging task than is presented by the Regal Lane agendas. This is a school that is apparently running very effectively, and where we have only let them know what the headmaster chooses to tell them. The headmaster should ideally be played by somebody who can present a competent and self-confident image, but perhaps also betray a touch of dismissiveness in his treatment of the governors. Their job is to try to show ways in which they *can* be helpful to him, not least in the disguised weak areas of the school.

TRAINING AGENDA NO 3

Papers to be Distributed to Students

PROSPECTUS

JOHN MILTON SCHOOL

Headmaster, T O Arnold, MA PhD

John Milton School is a school of some 1,300 pupils with a specialist staff of 90 teachers, together with non-teaching staff such as laboratory assistants, audio-visual aid technician, librarian, and matron. We believe that a large school can offer a variety of facilities as well as choice of subject that is not possible in a smaller school.

We aim to cater fully for every child no matter what the ability may be. We are as much concerned with the problems of the remedial child as with maintaining and increasing our fine record of examination successes. In this, results show we are abundantly succeeding.

We are concerned with the whole welfare of the pupil. The school is divided into four houses; the house remains the same throughout the whole of the school career. Houses are not merely a device for competitive games, drama festivals and assemblies; they are living and vital entities within the school that are meaningful and important to staff and pupils alike. We believe wholeheartedly in cooperation between school and parents, and, through a large number of formal and informal meetings, present abundant opportunity for parents to be involved in their child's education and in decisions affecting it.

The school has a large sixth form of about 143; this allows us to offer not only a full range of subjects at this level but also to form a sense of community within the sixth form which we consider is highly important to their development at this stage.

The teaching facilities of the school are excellent. The buildings are both modern and pleasant. There is language laboratory, a full range of science laboratories, a splendid music suite, a resource centre, senior and junior libraries, a mini-computer within the mathematics department; in short we are fully equipped both in terms of specialist teaching rooms and qualified and experienced staff to teach to all levels up to university entrance.

In our approach to teaching we are concerned with retaining the best of the traditional together with a cautious and carefully prepared introduction of new techniques. Thus we have the Cambridge classics foundation course in the first year, Nuffield physics and chemistry, new audio-visual language teaching, together with courses at fourth-year level for all students in social education, and computer experience in mathematics.

John Milton School is now a well-established all-ability school, with a fine record of academic success, an excellent staff, and a highly personal approach to the individual pupil.

The Curriculum

All pupils follow a common course in the first year, which includes the three sciences, a foreign language, drama, a classical studies foundation course and the basic subjects of secondary education. The common course continues for all pupils in the second and third years, with slight modifications; in particular those who are capable of benefiting from taking a second foreign language have the opportunity to do so.

During the third year pupils are able to select from 28 subjects the combinations they wish to take during the two years leading to GCE O Level or CSE. Throughout the period of decision, great care is taken to make sure that the right choice is made, and we expect that parents as well as children will be involved in consultation with staff, and especially with our full-time careers mistress.

A wide range of subjects is offered at the sixth-form level. The aim, again by detailed consultation, is to provide the most appropriate course for the individual student. In addition to the provision of 20 advanced-level subjects, we have a range of non advanced-level subjects which include, for example, study of art, geology, human biology, computer science, environmental studies, electronics, and home and community studies. Sixth-formers are also expected to follow a course of non-examination studies of a cultural nature.

Games

We have a full range of sports at the school. The boys play both soccer and rugby, as well as hockey and basketball. Cross-country running is increasing in popularity. In summer cricket and tennis are played, and there is a full programme of athletics. Swimming is possible for both boys and girls throughout the year. In winter the girls play hockey and netball; in summer they have tennis and athletics. In addition to these we can provide sailing, trampolining and volleyball for those who wish to take part. All pupils have physical education lessons in one of our two gymnasiums. There is a very full inter-house competition in most sports, and a full fixture list against other schools in the area.

Visits

A catalogue of visits and trips undertaken by members of the school will give some idea of the variety of interests catered for. Parties regularly visit local museums, factories, institutions and theatres. Every year the geography department takes senior pupils on field courses. Every year at least two parties visit a continental country. A recent innovation has been to send pupils in a particular year on residential courses, not only to work but also to get to know each other better.

Clubs and Societies

The school boasts a wide range of extra-curricular activities: in addition to the orchestra, various ensembles and choirs who give regular concerts, and a flourishing drama group, we have an astronomical society, a chess club, a Christian Union, a computer programming club, a debating society, Duke of Edinburgh Award schemes for boys and girls, an engineering club, a model railway club, a printing club, the roundabout club, and a woodwork club.

JOHN MILTON SCHOOL

GOVERNORS MEETING to be held at the school on 1 November at 6.00 pm.

AGENDA

1. Apologies for absence
2. Election of chairman
3. To receive the minutes of the last meeting held on 22 May (copy enclosed)
4. Matters arising
5. To receive the head's report
6. To fix dates for future meetings
7. Any other business

HEADMASTER'S REPORT

Staff The following staff left at the end of the Summer Term:

Name	Subject	Destination
Mr E Shaw	German/French	Retired
Mr F Leech	Head of History and Economics	Retired
Mrs C Coates	French teacher	Left teaching
Mr D Dickens	French teacher	Left teaching
Mr H Trevelyon	Head of sixth year	Head of Ysgol John Bugh Llandudno
Mr J Newman	Mathematics teacher	Moved to school in Bath
Mr D Churchill	French teacher	Grammar School, Dover
Miss G Wilde	English teacher	Retired
Miss J Lennon	Girls' PE	Head of Department, Culcheth High School, Cheshire
Mr K Soloman	School Counsellor	One year at Brunel to take Master of Technology Degree

The following staff joined the school in September, 1985:

Mr D Taylor	Geography	University of Durham
Miss J Heath	Girls' Physical Education	Anderson's School, Newcastle
Miss L Castle	German/French	Wall Hall College
Miss K Lane	Mathematics	Priestnaw High School, Harrow
Mr R Cecil	German/French	Durham and Reading Universities
Mr P Priestly	English	Rashleigh School, Sheffield
Mr W Hazel	French	Oxford University
Mr Grinwood	French	Portsmouth Poly and London Institute of Education
Mrs P Osborne	Biology Mrs Osborne did her teaching practice at John Milton	Newcastle University and London Institute of Education
Mrs M Bailey	French	Year in France
Mrs B Longford	English part-time	Temporary appointment

New members of staff seem to have settled into the school happily and quickly. Six are new to teaching after qualifying and four join us after experience in other schools.

The following internal promotions are made:

Mrs A E Parry to be Head of History and Economics
Mr R W Winston to be Head of Sixth Year

NUMBERS	Boys	Girls	Total
First year	130	102	232
Second year	140	110	250
Third year	122	126	248
Fourth year	125	110	235
Fifth year	129	112	241
Sixth year	72	71	143
	718	631	1349

EXAMINATION RESULTS, GENERAL CERTIFICATE OF EDUCATION AND CERTIFICATE OF SECONDARY EDUCATION, SUMMER

The advanced level results were exceptional; more individual subject passes were obtained than ever before. Two years ago there were 114 subject passes; last year there were 152, and this year 159. This was on a slightly lower entry than last year (216 compared to 233); the proportion of successes has also increased. There were 21 grade As compared with 16 last year, and 32 grade Bs compared with 15 last year. Plainly most subjects did well to attain such general results. However it might be worth mentioning English where 24 out of 24 passed with 5 grade As and 7 grade Bs. In physics 13 passed with 4 grade As.

At ordinary level there were 505 subject passes out of a total of 929. This is slightly down on last year; but it is significant to note that the percentage pass rate is still well above that of the last year of the grammar school (57% as compared to 48%). There were 32 grade A passes.

The number of candidates entered for CSE continues to grow: 212 this year compared to 200 last year and 166 the year before. The total number of examinations taken was 858; compared to 747 last year and 621 the year before. 117 grade 1s (which is the equivalent of a pass at ordinary level of the GCE) were gained, compared to 101 last year and 76 the year before. A total of 87% were graded. Chemistry and art and craft had the largest proportion of grade 1s. French results were very poor.

On the advanced level results on replies so far received, 17 pupils are proceeding to the universities, 5 arts and 12 sciences (three entries have been gained to Cambridge - one economist, one historian, one geographer) one to a polytechnic, eleven to colleges of education, eight to various professions.

STAFF ALLOWANCES

Allowances still continue to present a problem. We are still 10 points over our allocation of 73. We have had no success in getting a more generous allocation. This means that inevitably the balance of staffing is being shifted towards the inexperienced. As experienced staff leave they are inevitably replaced, unless they are in specific positions of responsibility, by teachers new to the profession. More serious still is the fact that when the teachers have served for two years in the school, they must look elsewhere for any promotion rather than within the school. This is an unhappy position.

I add a letter written by the chairman and the reply to this.

Mr T Gradgrind   10 June
Education Officer
County Hall
London SE1

Dear Mr Gradgrind

I am writing about the reduction of points allocated to the John
Milton School for graded posts. On the recent regrading the school
was allocated a points score of 73. This is 22 points lower than
the present number of points in use in the school.

I understand that the school's present unit total is 4,568. This
would place it very near the top range of a school in Group X1,
4,101–4,600, giving a points score range of 68–83. The allocation
of 73, in spite of the unit total, is well down the permitted range
under the current Burnham Report.

On the numbers at present in the school there is no question of the
school's unit total reducing before the next review. Totals moving
up the school are larger than those now in the fourth and fifth
years.

Plainly, to cut by as many as 20 points places the headmaster
under considerable pressure. I realise that he has been given
permission to offer allowances for certain key posts which have
recently become vacant, but he has also been told that he is
expected to cut his allowances to 73 as soon as possible.

This seems an obvious case in the light of the existing situation,
the rising numbers in the school, and the flexibility allowed in the
Burnham Report, for the school to be treated much more
generously than in the recent award.

Yours sincerely
I Chokechild
Chairman of Governors
J Milton School

REPLY:

Dear Mr Chokechild

Thank you for your letter which was received here on 12 July. The points score for the school has been assessed on the most generous basis available under the Burnham Report and in accordance with the Schools Sub-committee's scheme. There is more than one method of assessment allowed in the Burnham Report for a school in this situation and we have already taken the method which gives the best result.

The Schools Sub-committee did agree about a year ago that it would be desirable to increase the points available under the scheme but it was not possible to implement this improvement because of the budgetary situation. The situation has been no better this year of course – in fact it has been worse. The indications are that next year will also be very difficult and I would not be optimistic about the possibility of the points being increased.

Yours sincerely
T Gradgrind
Education Officer

SOCIAL EDUCATION

The following is an account of the social education scheme:

There were a number of elements that were considered to be essential components of the course. Careers was one of these. The head of the careers department had felt that to run independently in mixed-ability groups a course in careers timetabled weekly was an impossible task in terms of relevance to all pupils and that careers could have a more relevant and constructive contribution within the more flexible framework of a course in social education.

The course begins in the fourth year with a two-week introduction based on a contemporary social problem. Films like 'The Last Bus' or 'Sentence of the Court' are used. The aim at this stage is to involve pupils in meaningful discussions of a theme based on incidents well within their comprehension. The rest of the first term is spent on two themes – conservation and consumer education. The second term begins with an introduction to local government and continues with individual and group surveys of various aspects – housing, social services, planning, transport, education, leisure. The term ends with a mock council meeting. The first half of the third term is given over to careers. Pupils complete a school careers form and an interest questionnaire. They are then placed in broad interest groups, in which further careers lessons take place. At the end of this term they have a course on some of the social, moral and religious implications of our society, and these are worked out in an examination of our attitudes to christenings, weddings and funerals.

During this year pupils are withdrawn for half a term in single-sex groups for the showing of informative films, film-strips and slides on sexual intercourse, procreation, venereal disease and personal relationships. These are followed by discussions led by members of staff who have been sepecially selected for this aspect of the course. Great thought is given to the level of information and approaches through discussions with gynaecologists, marriage-guidance workers and the examination of visual aids and books available. This is undertaken by the teaching group. The contact is through the teachers in the group and not through outside speakers. We regard this as important in terms of establishing an atmosphere not only where full and frank information can be given but also where questions can be asked and problems brought into the open without embarrassment or hesitation. A meeting is held for parents at which they are told what we are doing and shown the audio-visual materials which are used. This work continues into the fifth year with the same groups.

The average size of a group is 15; this makes discussion informal and constructive and allows groups to be taken out in the school minibus. From the outset we were determined to have mixed-ability groups. As far as possible groups are formed from house tutor groups which were the the teaching unit in the first year, in some subjects in the second and third years, and which meet together several times a week throughout the five/seven-year period of schooling. There are problems of presenting themes in such a way that the less able are not swamped by abstract intellectual theory. However, in discussion it is often the more able who need encouragement in voicing their inner feelings or in asking questions. The less academic often show more initiative in person-to-person research or in work with younger or handicapped children. One result of this bringing together of all pupils in mixed-ability groups to consider topics outside the accepted school curriculum has been a greater degree of social integration; it has given some impetus to a continuing identity with the school of all pupils in their fourth and fifth years.

Inevitably an account like this gives the impression that the scheme ran smoothly and has evolved an entirely satisfying and acceptable framework. In practice we have been frequently dissatisfied with some aspects and with some approaches. We are constantly rethinking and re-planning. The flexibility of approach enables us to subtract from or add to the scheme without upsetting our faith, our aims and our sense of purpose. Where formerly we felt worried about neglecting or dealing only spasmodically or fragmentarily with this complex field, we now have a framework in which we can present and develop what we feel is essential in the light of the changing needs of our pupils and society and of our own experience gained from the scheme itself.

REPORT OF A HEAD OF HOUSE

This report of a head of house is included unedited. A considered impression of the development of the house through games, social activities and assemblies, rather than a recording of events that have taken place during the year, was suggested.

Two of the main tasks of the house are (i) to develop as a social unit within which the individual develops a sense of belonging, and (ii) to encourage individual pupils to develop their talents and personalities to the full.

(i) The development of the social unit

(a) House Assemblies   The house assembly, which takes place on alternate days, is an essential part of house life. It presents the opportunity to pupils and staff of meeting together as a social unit and it acts as an essential vehicle of communication. It has developed in a number of ways. Some have followed traditional lines, others have included music and drama items, while others have been taken by individual pupils or individual form groups (first to sixth). This involvement of the pupils is working well, and is proving much more interesting and effective to the majority. The pupils are encouraged to select a topic relevant to a particular theme, eg people of other lands or a specific topic of particular interest to themselves.

(b) House Period   The greatest opportunity to develop the personal contact is within the house period. We have attempted to lay down certain guidelines for the form tutor to follow. Basically it should be a time when a pupil can discuss particular problems with the tutor (and vice versa), or an opportunity for the form tutor to organise group activities. One or two sixth formers have been allocated to junior forms and they have been invaluable in helping to establish personal contact with individuals. The success of the house period has varied according to the interest taken in it by the form tutor, but I felt that a general improvement had been made during the last year.

Next year we hope to develop close links with the careers department, so that more information and instruction about careers can be given, particularly to forms 3 to 6. It will also involve the form tutor more closely in the future of each pupil.

In the weekly house period of the first year forms with the head of house, links have been set up between John Milton School and a school in Bhilwara, NW India. This has been and is being expanded with stories about India and the collection of information about the country.

(c) The House Council   For just over one year the house council has been functioning successfully. For most of this time it has acted as a forum for the exchange of ideas and the discussion of problems relating to the school. Now that a school council is established, the house council will discuss matters relating only to the house.

(d) <u>Problem Children</u>   As much time as possible is spent in counselling problem children, either at form tutor or at head of house level. In order to keep in touch with many of these, either the deputy or the head of house supervises the weekly detention, and persistent offenders are checked through a conduct report which is signed by teachers at each lesson. As much contact as possible is maintained with parents, through individual interviews, telephone conversations, and parents' evenings. A weekly meeting is held with a member of the school welfare department, so that specific children, or general problems can be discussed. This has proved invaluable in achieving financial help for children of poor home backgrounds. Links are also maintained with child guidance.

(e) <u>Social Activities</u>   Ideally, various sections of the house should be able to meet socially in a less formal way at some time. Unfortunately this has not been possible to organise on a large scale yet, except in the form of an upper sixth party, and a social holiday for the first form. The social holiday is being organised for the end of June at a holiday fellowship camp, at Staithes in Yorkshire.

(ii)   <u>Opportunity for the development of individual talent</u>
(a) Games   In sporting activities there have been few match successes, but there has been a general improvement in attitude during the year. The overall efficiency of team selection has been improved by the establishment of a sports council.

(b) <u>Other Activities</u>   There has been a keen interest in drama, and a junior drama club has been firmly established to produce plays, not only for the house competition, but also for house assemblies. Other clubs and activities have been encouraged, and a number of pupils have initiated school clubs, eg cycling and fishing.

Conclusion

In the final analysis, the success or failure of the house in giving the child a sense of belonging depends greatly on the teaching staff within the house. A considerable amount of hard work is spent by them in achieving this objective and for this I am very grateful.

VISITS OF STUDENTS FROM COKETOWN COLLEGE OF TECHNOLOGY

Two students from Coketown College of Technology visited the school on Wednesday 4 May during the lunch hour, without first seeking my permission. I wrote to the principal of Coketown College of Technology about this incident. I add a copy of this letter and Dr Clark's reply.

Dr G S Clark   10 May
Coketown College of Technology
London NW2

Dear Mr Clark,

I am writing about two of the students from Coketown College of Technology who visited this school during the lunchtime of Wednesday, 4th May. They were members of the RSSF (Socialist Society). They spoke to the sixth form students and distributed leaflets. They came into school without seeking permission and without making their presence known to me or to any other member of the staff. I regard this as an act of discourtesy on their part, and I should be grateful if my attitude on this point could be made known to them.

Yours sincerely
T O Arnold

T O Arnold, Esq, MA, PhD   16 May
Headmaster
John Milton School
London NW6

Dear Dr Arnold,

Thank you for your letter of 10 May. I too regard it as an act of discourtesy that anyone should visit your school without seeking appropriate permission and I have so informed the students' union.

The difficulty I face is that facing many institutions of higher education, the malaise in which will be well known to you. But you may be interested to learn that

(a)   the visit was carried out without the knowledge or backing of the students' union.

(b)   the 'militant' students involved in the RSSF number about 30 out of a total student body of 1,350.

Apart from expressing my distaste for the students' action, I have no effective recourse. It is, however, a matter of conjecture how long such an unsatisfactory state of affairs will be generally condoned. There are signs of growing backlash from both staff and students, and more important, from the general public.

Yours sincerely
G S Clark, Principal, OBE, TD, PhD, DFH, Hon MIIED, C Eng, FIMA, FIEE

A report of this visit appeared in the local press. Subsequently, three students from Coketown College, including the two who had made the previous visit, called on me. I had a discussion with them about their previous visit and the question of their 'trespassing' in the school. The attitude of the sixth form here is perhaps best expressed in a letter that two of them wrote in answer to the report in the local press.

Sixth-Formers' Protest

We, as sixth-formers of John Milton School, resent Mr Hugh Maguire's implication that it is necessary to protect us from exponents of extremist politics.

The idea that our outlook on politics should be swayed by two radical students in the space of 40 minutes, seems to us ridiculous.

Many leaving school this year will be thrown into the heart of university politics, where they will be subject to various shades of student opinion. Surely, it is the function of schools, and especially the sixth forms, to produce students who are capable of independent thought on political as well as other issues.

We would like to think that we are capable of considering critically ideas presented to us, and should regard it as laughable if the police had to be called to protect us from the opinions laid in front of us.

Nick Baker,
Martin Lynch.

The question for the future is whether to permit these visits. I have so far allowed this group to make one visit. My own attitude is that, within limits and not during actual school hours, the sixth form should be allowed – subject to my permission – to have visitors in their common room if they are invited and if they observe the necessary previous formalities. The majority of our sixth form are not going to be swayed one way or the other by such visits. In any case, many of them will soon be subject to such ideas in a few months' time at university or institutions of higher education, and it is unrealistic to seek to protect them from different shades of student opinion during the time they are at school.

By banning such visits a situation might well be created in the sixth form; it is no use speaking to them of responsibility at one time and then treating them differently over issues like this – especially when there is no indication that they are anything but critical of the ideas that these students presented to them. I am considering the possibility of holding a forum in the school on the present student crisis and the problem of authority which would represent all shades of opinion.

SUSPENSION OF A PUPIL

I suspended a pupil, Jane Thomas, from school from Tuesday 17 May until the end of term three days later. The reason for this was that she attacked a teacher in the lower school on Monday 16 May. The teacher threatened to confiscate a radio that she was apparently playing during the lesson. Jane then took the teacher's bag and said she could not have it back until she gave the radio back to her. Then they exchanged blows until, according to the girl, she gave up because the teacher was in tears. The teacher concerned was Mrs Wilson who teaches here on Mondays in place of Mr Clark who is attending a course on Mondays. The girl has previously been in a substantial amount of trouble in school, has been in court recently, and is on probation. I was in contact with Mrs Thomas on the Monday about the whole question of Jane and about the suspension. The parents accepted that the suspension in the circumstances was very reasonable.

This was Mrs Wilson's last day as a teacher in the school. The girl's conduct has improved since she returned to school this term.

FIRST YEAR QUESTIONNAIRE

In the summer we set a questionnaire to 212 first-year pupils. They were allowed, if they wished, to answer anonymously in order to encourage the uninhibited expression of their ideas and feelings.

The first question we asked was how long it took to find their way around the school. Only three took longer than four weeks; the majority had sorted out this problem during the first week and 20 in the first two days. Of course, we go to considerable lengths to help them in this with plans, guided tours in the term before they come, and explanations from house form tutors in the first two days. We asked how helpful they found members of staff, particularly associated with them, in helping them to settle in the school; the replies were very disappointing. Only about a third had found staff helpful here. It may be that children in a new school are shy at approaching any member of staff, and it may well be that the substantial amount of formal help in time allotted to house form tutors was not considered 'help'. They had incidentally met these house form tutors at a special meeting in the summer term whilst their parents were in a separate meeting.

About half had found older pupils helpful but only 13 had found sixth-formers helpful.

We asked them a number of questions about school subjects in which we discovered without surprise that there is very high correlation between liking a subject and success in it – with the exception of games which a large number liked yet considered themselves not very successful at. Asked what aspects of school they enjoyed most – 144 answered sport; school journeys, new friends, individual subjects gained between 30 and 40 votes; clubs and house competitions (music, drama and sport) had about 20 votes. One said 'all of it' and some humorists said break and holidays.

A question on homework showed that the majority were spending less time on it than the school expected. There are, of course, problems in setting homework in the first year in subjects such as the Nuffield sciences and audio-visual language teaching. A large majority thought homework had helped them, chiefly as an aid to learning. Only 17 thought it encouraged individual thought and only four thought that they were helped by parental aid. We have school uniform and 136 agreed with compulsory school uniform as against 71 who were opposed to it. The same number (136) wanted to see changes in it; 16 were against change. There is a periodic review of uniform here where the opinions of pupils, parents and staff are fully considered. Some wanted a particular fashion such as denim skirts to become uniform. T-shirts, training shoes and wider choices of colour were frequent demands. A majority had found no cause for unhappiness in school during the first year. One cause mentioned was bullying (something that we are very vigilant about and we take very prompt and decisive action even in slight cases). We were alarmed that 31 mentioned it. Jostling in queues (chiefly the school tuck shop) was mentioned by 10; unjust discipline and too much homework by 5; loss of friends by 4; individual teachers were mentioned by 20.

Asked about improvements in the school, most mentioned facilities such as more drinking fountains, benches, a swimming bath and a miscellaneous collection ranging from clocks in classrooms, stricter teachers, fewer detentions to fewer double lessons.

The advice they would give to a new boy or girl was to behave well (46), not to worry (23), to do homework (17), to work hard (20), to beware of bullies (9), ask if lost (7), be polite to staff (22), listen to teachers (7), be neatly dressed (9), get a plan of the school (5), make friends (5), beware of strict teachers (8).

193 thought that their parents were pleased that they were at this school. 110 had different friends from those in their previous school and 63 still had the same friends. The majority were aware of the existence of a junior school council; 16, astonishingly since time is given in house tutor time to preparing for, and reporting back on, meetings, did not know we had one. 134 thought it was for discussion, 28 to debate improvements, 8 for new ideas, 13 did not know what it was for, and surprisingly only 9 thought it was for complaints.

The final question was about ways, if any, in which they thought they might have done better in the first year. 59 decided they might have concentrated more or worked harder; 18 might have behaved better; 4 might have improved their spelling; 7 might have had more confidence.

What is the value of these answers? They jolted our complacency considerably in some aspects in which we considered we had an outstanding record. We made considerable enquiries for instance about the question of bullying which 31 said had caused them unhappiness in school during the year. To some extent, this underlined the problem of definition to which all surveys are subject.

We learnt a lot about definition of questions in order to clarify answers in future surveys. However, in some respects, there is something to be said for not making such a survey too rigid in its definitions. Misinterpretation of a question may be illuminating.

Above all, it is an attempt to explore the mind of the consumer in the school, the pupil, and this is its real value.

UNIFORM

Uniform committee meetings were held during last term. There was no demand for any significant changes in the boys' uniform. I add the report of the girls' uniform committee meetings. Items 2 and 3 of the meeting held on 24 May are the ones which need a decision. I would have no objection to this permission being given.

Girls Uniform Committee Meeting held on 3 May

Mrs Perry stated that any proposals for the uniform change would have to be put to the headmaster, for consideration by him, the governors and the parents.

The first matter raised was a change in winter school uniform to trousers, polo-necked sweaters and a smock top. After discussion, it was concluded that the smock top is a passing phase in fashion and not suited to many girls. The idea of a sweater next to the skin was rejected as it would not fill the requirements of freshness and ease of washing as the school blouse does. The idea of trouser suits as uniform was raised but it was decided that many styles did not suit all girls and the expense of a good tailored suit would be far too great. Other than a blouse under a sweater with trousers, no other ideas came forward for tops to match the trousers.

Identification of houses also posed a problem. Sweaters in house colours, blouses in house colours and seams of trousers in house colours were rejected. The use of house badges for identification was accepted. So the first decision of the meeting was that house forms should discuss the colour, design and materials for the proposed winter uniform.

Another aspect of winter uniform raised was that of outdoor coats. The blue gaberdine raincoat is now considered rather old-fashioned.

However, the range of colours and styles of many of the outdoor coats worn by pupils was considered to be well outside the limits of any uniform regulation. A suggestion was made that the coats should be in one dark colour or a choice of two or three dark colours. This was referred to house forms for discussion.

The last item of the meeting was summer uniform. After discussion it was proposed that there should be no change in summer uniform.

Girls' Uniform Committee Meeting held on 24 May

1. After reporting back on discussions with the forms the conclusion was that the majority of girls preferred blouses underneath the pullover to go with the trousers. Also preferred was the idea of badges for house identification rather than ties.
2. It was agreed that black trousers for winter should be accepted as an optional alternative to the school skirt.
3. Having discussed the proposed winter uniform fully, Mrs Perry agreed she would ask the headmaster to consider a girls' winter uniform of black trousers with a blouse under the present school pullover with a house badge or tie.
4. The situation concerning school winter coats was raised once again with the decision that coats should be in a plain dark colour, eg black, navy blue or dark green.
5. School shoes were the next matter raised. Here it was agreed that platform shoes will soon pass out of fashion and that shoes should be in a dark colour, eg black or brown. Mrs Perry mentioned, at this point, that she did not mind reasonable, sensible shoes but she would be clamping down on shoes likely to endanger health.
6. Finally it was agreed that blazers should be worn in summer and not ordinary, highly coloured, fashionable jackets.

John Milton School Uniform

GIRLS

Plain grey or black skirt
Plain white shirt-blouse
Long-sleeved, v-necked pullover in plain grey or black
Black blazer (badge obtainable only from school)
House tie (obtainable from head of house)
Sensible, low-heeled walking shoes in plain brown or black
Black or beige nylon tights or grey or white socks
Plain grey, black or navy outdoor coat or raincoat or
plain grey, black or navy or khaki anorak or parka
Plain black trousers (not cords or denims) may be worn in winter
months after half-term in the autumn

Physical Education
Cellular shirt, open-necked type, in house colour
Terylene-rayon, grey pleated and kilt-type skirt
White socks
White plimsolls
Black athletic shorts (striped in house colours from PE mistress)
Hockey boots
Grey hockey socks
Regulation black swimsuit and red cap
A towel for showers
A track suit may be worn for athletics and sport in winter
'Whites' or games kit may be worn for tennis

ALL ITEMS MUST BE CLEARLY NAMED

BOYS

Plain grey or black trousers
Black blazer (badge obtainable only from head of house)
or dark plain grey, black or navy suit
Plain grey or white shirt
Plain grey or black, v-necked pullover
House tie (obtainable from head of house)
Plain dark grey, black or navy socks
Sensible low-heeled walking shoes in plain brown or black
Plain grey, black or navy outdoor coat or raincoat or
plain grey, black, navy or khaki anorak or parka

Physical Education
Football shirt in school colours ⎫
Rugby shirt in house colour   ⎬ both shirts necessary
                                ⎭
Football boots
White football stockings
TWO pairs white shorts (necessary because of quantity of physical work)
White gym shoes
Towel for showers
White shirt for cricket
School cricket team players will need white trousers or shorts for matches
Swimming trunks

ALL ITEMS MUST BE CLEARLY NAMED

Appendix C
Possible Questions Arising out of Training Agenda No 1

Head's Report – Item (2a) Accommodation

Possible questions to be asked by the governors:

- Why has the roll risen? Is it growing population, or popularity, or both?
- Is the local population rising? How can we find out?
- Are there any more plans for housing development in the area? How can we find out?
- Is the nearest school full?
- Does the present accommodation infringe the Schools Regulations of space per child?
- What is the authority's class size policy? Is this school keeping to it?
- Is there no question of the deputy taking a class?
- What are the numbers of children in each age group?
- How should the governors go about trying to get a new school or mobile classroom? Is there room in the playground? (but see item 4)
- In the meantime how can the numbers be contained? Should the school have a catchment area?
- What priority should be given to admitting the 'halfway house' children, even if it means overcrowding?
- Are there any facilities in the neighbourhood that could be made use of to relieve pressure?
- How are admissions dealt with?
- Is there any liaison with the social service department about the new families in the terrace across the road? (see item (e)).
- Should we ask for another teacher?

Possible action to be taken:
- Pass a resolution asking for temporary accommodation (see item 4).
- Set up a working party to investigate likely future need.
- Ask for a report on the liaison between the education, housing

and social services committees in respect of the
developments in the area.
- Ask the head teacher to consult with his staff about the
possibility of rearranging classes so as to distribute numbers
more evenly?*
- Ask the authority to impose a catchment area, in consultation
with the governors.
- Ask for a deputation of governors to go and see the officer or
committee chairman in charge of building and
accommodation.
- Ask for a letter to be written to the local councillor inviting
him or her to visit the school and take the matter up.
- Ask for another special meeting within a specific time to
receive an account of whatever progress has been made.
- Ask for an extra teacher to help in taking groups out of
classrooms for special work.

Head's Report – Item (2b) Teaching Staff

Possible questions:
- Is not there a rather high percentage of probationers? What
sort of support is being organised for them, both by the
authority and within the school?
- How were the decisions reached as to what the responsibility
posts would be for?
- Does any teacher take responsibility for mathematics
throughout the school?
- Who is responsible for girls' games?
- Could Mrs Power's job involve liaison with social services etc
over the problem families in halfway housing?
- Do we necessarily want to use the remaining scale point
now? (Next year the three probationers would be eligible for
it, and it is possible that one of them might be more useful
for the school than Mrs Howard.)
- Could we not get more remedial help, with the new influx of
children needing it?
- Why has the additional Burnham point only just come to our
notice? (We might not have lost three teachers if it had been
used last year.)

Possible action:
- Ask for a ruling about holding a point over.
- Ask for a report from the LEA on support for probationers.

---

* The average class in this school is about 31. Obviously than some classes are much bigger than
others, if some are over 35.

- Ask for a future opportunity to discuss the areas of work that are the responsiblities of the scale post holders.
- Ask the LEA for more remedial teaching help.
- Ask for a report on the possibility of the school having another Burnham point.

Note to Instructor

During this discussion, you could point out that this is a very good opportunity to discuss the actual work and curriculum of the school, but it needs handling with some tact. Every one of the questions, for instance, could be an extremely sensitive one. You could discuss ways of getting information while still appearing helpful and supportive – and indeed being so. The point of getting full information about the school is not simply the governors' 'right to know' (although this is a factor), but to help the effective functioning of the school in any way possible.

On last paragraph (Music)
- Can the authority's music inspector not help in finding a woodwind teacher?
- Where has Mrs Smith tried to find a woodwind teacher? Are there possibly other places to advertise?
- If we do get more music teaching time, will it be at the expense of other parts of the school curriculum, or can the school have it as an extra?
- Has parental support been sought in the musical activities?
- Are the 'very musical' children getting music teaching at the expense of the music education of the others?

Head's Report – Item (2c) School Meals

Possible questions:
- Is the head satisfied that all those entitled to free dinners receive them?
- Are those receiving free school dinners made to feel 'different'?
- How does our percentage of free meals compare with the authority's average?
- Would there be a possibility of advertising for kitchen staff locally, in corner shops etc?
- Are there any suggestions that the school meals service could endeavour to make the food more appealing to the children? Have the children or their parents been asked for suggestions?

Possible action:
- Ask for the governors to be sent the regulations regarding free school meals, and the ways in which entitlement is claimed, so that they can suggest ways of making it better known locally.
- Ask permission to advertise for kitchen staff.
- Set up working party to suggest possible changes of menu.

Note to Instructor

This is an item on which a lot of time can be spent rather unproductively. It is probably an instance where a small working party of governors coming in to see, and taste, the school meals will achieve more than a lengthy committee discussion.

Head's Report – Item (2d) Improvements

Possible questions:
- How long have we been waiting for the shelves? What excuse has been given? What action by the governors might end the delay? Has the chairman contacted the relevant office?
- Is it not possible for a parent or the caretaker to fix the display boarding? Does the head think there is any danger in leaving it stacked?
- How much would installing the sinks cost? Is there any special fund which could be tapped for carrying out this work? Alternatively, could the school raise the money itself?

Possible action:
- Ask for a ruling by the authority on volunteer work on minor maintenance and improvement work.
- Ask for permission, and an allowance for, contracting small building jobs out locally.
- Pass a resolution condemning the delay.
- Ask for a list of the special funds set up by the authority, and the purpose of each.
- Set up a working party to consult with the PTA about raising money for this sort of improvement.
- Ask for a site meeting with the officer responsible for small maintenance and improvement work.
- Invite the caretaker to the next meeting to discuss these matters.

Head's Report – Item (2e) Other Reports

Transfer

Possible questions:
- What is the liaison between this school and the secondary schools it feeds?
- Did all these children get the school of first choice? If not, why not?
- What is the history of the child who went to the school for children with behavioural problems? Should he have gone earlier?

Possible action:
(Depends very much on the answers produced by the head to the questions, which can be varied according to local circumstances. They could reveal malfunctioning of the transfer system as such, lack of liaison between schools, discriminatory practices by some secondary schools, delays in assessment of children for special education etc. Action should address itself to finding out about and correcting any of these factors.)

School Journey

Possible questions:
- Why did the three who stayed behind not go?
- What did they do at school during this time?
- How much did the school journey cost?
- What subsidy was available, either for individuals or for the group?

Possible action:
- Look at the offered account, and offer congratulations and suggestions. (Very important to do this seriously.)
- Find out about possible extra funding for needy children.

Confidential Item

Possible questions:
- Is it right that governors should not normally be 'troubled' with this sort of problem?
- In what way did the head 'question' John? Should he have done so, without contacting the parents?
- What sort of support are the families in the halfway houses receiving from social services or other agencies such as the education welfare service?

- Is John in need of psychiatric help? Is any teacher particularly involved with him and his family? What educational standard has he reached?
- Are the local police known to the children and the school personnel on a friendly neighbourhood basis?
- Do relations between shops and the school need improving? Could local governors help in this?
- What part does the school see itself playing in the developing tension between different elements in the community? Could it play a positive reconciling role? How?

Possible action:
- Ask for meeting with social services and/or housing department, and/or local councillors to initiate liaison over local problems.
- Take initiative in suggesting school as base for community activity that might ease conflict. (A function in collaboration with PTA.)
- Ask for further report on help given to John and his family, by services at the disposal of the education department.

Item 3 School Allowance

On this item particularly, local arrangements and yearly budgets vary so wildly that a local and topical example of how the school allowance figures are set out is essential. We include these figures as an example of one time and one place only: however the questions below may indicate possible areas of discussion.

Possible questions:
- What was the major equipment?
- Does the head have complete discretion within the overall figure?
- What consultation takes place within the school?
- What is the 'prize' money spent on?
- Is there enough for activities and amenities (this presumably means outings).
- Can the governors appeal for more money, for special circumstances?
- Who chooses the books?
- What is included in the first item?
- Is there any way of saving on consumables? (Link-up with local printers for off-cuts, for instance.)
- Are these figures already committed? In other words, is the governors' approval merely formal?

- Is there in addition a school fund, based on voluntary contributions and fund raising? Who administers it? Would it be possible for the governors to see the accounts?

Item 4 Nursery Class

The instructor should introduce this item by referring to discussion and decisions (which we must assume to have happened) about the proposed nursery. The attached plans should be presented for the governors' approval. (They are in fact standard plans drawn up by the ILEA for new nursery class buildings.)

There are no particular catches or defects that we know of in the design, though governors should be invited to query anything they are dubious about. They should be expected for instance to ask about the dividers between the two main areas, and between play area and quiet area, about the position of the block in relation to the school, about the outside play area, and about access. They should also try to make sure that the head, or the nursery teacher appointed if there is one, is consulted about as much of the final stages as possible. In all the questioning the clerk will have to improvise answers; those who are diffident about their competence in this field should remember first that the quality of the questions is more important than that of the answers, and also that of course in real life the clerk would not be an architectural expert anyway, and is likely to fall back on replying, 'I'll have to refer that question to the architect'. If the 'governors' are very dissatisfied, this should lead them to request a meeting on site with the architect. For further comment on this item read Chapter 6 on Accommodation in the Handbook.

Apart from comment and question on the design it would be natural at this stage to have discussion of what else needs to be done in relation to the opening of the nursery. When will it be open? How will it be publicised? What will be the criteria for admission? If there is no time for such a discussion, somebody should propose that it goes on the agenda for the next meeting.

Item 5 Visiting Governors

You may not ever reach this item! However, if you have given yourself plenty of time and find that you do, you should between you have evolved an imaginary school in which the item may be an interesting or delicate one in any of a number of ways. You can open the item by asking the head if any governors have visited since the last meeting, and you can concoct a story beforehand with him – either that the head thinks visits other than to attend formal functions unnecessary and has consistently discouraged them, or that none of the governors has bothered to visit, or that too many governors have been visiting and upsetting the staff. You can also ask individual governors to report on their visits. In any case, this item can be used for raising, discussing and deciding on what sort of visits would be acceptable and useful, and arranging who will undertake them and when.

Also, see advice in Chapter 15 of the Handbook.

Item 6 Date of Next Meeting

See advice in Chapter 6 of the Handbook on the Agenda.

Item 7 Other Urgent Business

Maybe by this stage, governors are bursting with unanswered worries about the school which they want to bring up, and items which they want discussed some time in the future. We hope that somewhere they will have picked up the restricted school site (now to have a nursery in it as well) and the outside lavatories! But see the advice on this item in Chapter 6 of the Handbook.

Appendix D
Character Notes for Agenda No 2

(To be given initially only to those playing the parts of the candidates, and then discussed by all the 'governors' after the 'appointment' has been made.)

Character Sketch of Frances Holmes

She is a brilliant and dedicated teacher, believing passionately in the need to stimulate intellectual activity in urban children by taking them out of the classroom, and setting very high standards for herself and her pupils. Her class's work has been nationally exhibited, and was quite exceptional. She has attended a great number of courses on all subjects, and in the last year contributed two lectures to one herself, at the request of her district inspector.

She had no trouble with discipline or organisation from the start, and as a result has given very little thought to the problems of the average probationary teacher. Her superiors – most of them – recognise her as a rising star; her present head feels he is extremely lucky to have had her for four years. The charisma she has for the children also works for some of the younger teachers, though others are frightened of her. She took her responsibility for arranging educational visits very seriously and did not always avoid offending other teachers by appearing to interfere with their work. At least one teacher left as a result.

She lives alone, rather a long journey away from the area where she works. She intends to move further in, but never has time to look for a room. She has not many outside interests, but is completely, almost fanatically sometimes, involved in activities connected with teaching. Physically she is not very strong, and does not always realise when she is wearing herself out. She was in hospital for three weeks last winter with pneumonia. Her doctor told her it was brought on by nervous exhaustion, but she did not believe him.

She has no experience of administrative detail and is rather contemptuous of 'form-filling'. However, she clearly has the ability to master the techniques necessary.

Her weaknesses are: her health, coupled with the long journey; her lack of understanding of younger teachers; her youth, possibly.

Character Sketch of Mary Power

She lives within walking distance of the school and is very much part of the neighbourhood. She had three years' teaching experience before she got married, then left work although she did not have any children until three years later, when she had twin sons. Both children were very frail for a number of years, started school late and needed a lot of support and encouragement; Mrs Power did not go back to teaching until they started secondary school. Both are now 16, doing very well and are heading for university. During the years she was not working she became very active in local affairs (see her application). Her abiding interest is understandably her two sons.

She is popular with staff and children. She has a very relaxed air, and is guided in her teaching by the motherly instinct which has been so well exercised in her own family. She finds it hard to take an interest in the theory of education and in staffroom discussions on this sort of subject she tends to be silent.

She is not naturally ambitious, but last year her husband had a serious heart attack, and she is worried now at the prospect of possibly being the sole earner during the period her sons are at university. This is why she is seeking promotion.

She is probably competent at administration, but has not yet been tried. Although she is warm-hearted, she is uneasy about the local council's action in putting so many problem families into the area: she feels slightly threatened as a local resident. This, and her only moderately committed attitude to teaching, are her chief weaknesses as a candidate for this job.

Character Sketch of Ian Walton

He is an excellent organiser with a reputation for seeing that things get done. He is very keen on sport and much admired by the children for his prowess and the way he coaches the football team. He has made the complexities of operating a school on a split site as easy as possible for the staff and is very sensitive to the need of teachers for a satisfactory working environment; he has realised, for instance, the need to get the cooperation of the caretaking staff (and has got it). However, because he is so good at all of this, he often underestimates the importance of what is actually being taught, and is less help to younger teachers on curriculum and content than he is on discipline and management.

He is married to a teacher, who is at present five months pregnant. They live in a two-room furnished flat for which they pay £50 a week. His wife plans to give up teaching when the baby is born, and the couple then plan to live as frugally as they can until he can get a house and a headship somewhere in the country. He reckons that it is fair to give two years to this job, if he gets it, and he will be unwilling to offer more. He would also be unwilling, if really hard pressed, to promise even that long. If something suitable came along after a year, he obviously might be tempted.

The gap between 1978 and 1980 in Mr Walton's application is explained in the following way. Although he passed the practical part of his college of education course, he failed some of the academic papers twice. This very much shook him at the time and he did in fact 'drift' for 18 months or so, doing a number of casual jobs, before pulling himself together and finally re-sitting and passing. This experience in no way invalidates his suitability for the job, but the fact that he is still somewhat humiliated by what he sees as a blot on his career and has tried to keep it off the application form may say something about his character.

His main weaknesses as an applicant are the likelihood that he will move on soon, and his lack of imagination about the curriculum.